Building Foundations: Building a Place for God's Glory

Building a Place for God's Glory
Based on the Pattern of the Tabernacle of Moses

Building Foundations: A Spirit Filled Children's Church Curriculum

Pastor Tamera Kraft
Revival Fire 4 Kids Resource

Mt Zion Ridge Press LLC
295 Gum Springs Rd, NW
Georgetown, TN 37366

https://www.mtzionridgepress.com

Copyright © 2020 by Mt Zion Ridge Press
ISBN 13: 978-1-949564-83-9

Published in the United States of America
Publication Date: February 14, 2020

Editor-In-Chief: Michelle Levigne
Executive Editor: Tamera Lynn Kraft

Cover Art Copyright by Tamera Lynn Kraft and Mt Zion Ridge Press LLC © 2020

All rights reserved. No portion of this book may be reproduced or transmitted in any form or by any electronic or mechanical means, including photocopying, recording or by any information retrieval and storage system without permission of the publisher.

Pirating of books is illegal. Criminal Copyright Infringement, *including* infringement without monetary gain, may be investigated by the Federal Bureau of Investigation and is punishable by up to five years in federal prison and a fine of up to $250,000.

Copyright permissions for this curriculum: When you register this curriculum, you are granted permission to make as many copies as needed for the use of the church or ministry registered only. *Do not distribute this material to other churches or ministries without permission. Copying materials in any other way violates copyright laws.*

For questions about copyright issues or other matter concerning rights for this curriculum, contact revivalfire4kids@att.net.

Building Foundations Curriculum is a Revival Fire for Kids resource. For more information about Revival Fire for Kids, check out their website at http://revivalfire4kids.net

Registration and Digital Files (Available for FREE with purchase of the curriculum): Digital files (jpeg graphics, video clips, other resources) are available to anyone who purchases and registers this curriculum at no additional cost. To register, click on this link http://eepurl.com/glsELH or type it in the address box on your browser and fill out the form. We never sell or give away any information we receive.

DVD: If you prefer a DVD of Jpeg images and video clips, you may purchase it at http://mtzionridgepress.com for an additional cost.

Building a Place for God's Glory is available in PDF download and print and includes 13 lessons and is available in PDF download or print.

All Scripture in this curriculum is from the NIV (2011) Bible unless otherwise designated.

THE HOLY BIBLE, NEW INTERNATIONAL VERSION®, NIV® Copyright © 1973, 1978, 1984, 2011 by Biblica, Inc.® Used by permission. All rights reserved worldwide.

Some Scripture is also used from these versions:

THE HOLY BIBLE, INTERNATIONAL CHILDREN'S BIBLE® ICB Copyright© 1986, 1988, 1999, 2015 by Tommy Nelson™, a division of Thomas Nelson. Thomas Nelson is a registered trademark of HarperCollins Christian Publishing, Inc.

NEW KING JAMES VERSION® NKJV® Scripture taken from the New King James Version®. Copyright © 1982 by Thomas Nelson. Used by permission. All rights reserved.

Building a Place for God's Glory © Mt Zion Ridge Press, 2020. All rights reserved.

Copyright permissions for this curriculum: When you register this curriculum, you are granted permission to make as many copies as needed for the use of the church or ministry registered only. *Do not distribute this material to other churches or ministries without permission. Copying materials in any other way violates copyright laws.*

For questions about copyright issues or other matter concerning rights for this curriculum, contact revivalfire4kids@att.net.

Building Foundations Curriculum is a Revival Fire for Kids resource. For more information about Revival Fire for Kids, check out their website at http://revivalfire4kids.net

Materials included:

13 complete downloadable lessons including 26 object lessons, 13 skits, 13 games, 13 Bible Stories, 13 memory verse activities, graphics to be used in PowerPoint slides for 13 lessons, 13 small group discussions, and 13 Family Devotion Handouts. The lessons and graphics will be available for immediate download.

Table of Contents

How to Use this Curriculum

Lesson 1: Prepare to Enter God's Presence   pg. 1
Psalm 100:4 *Enter His gates with thanksgiving and His courts with praise; give thanks to Him and praise His name.*

Lesson 2: The Fire that Forgives   pg. 11
Repent therefore and be converted, that your sins may be blotted out, so that times of refreshing may come from the presence of the Lord. Acts 3:19 NKJV

Lesson 3: Clean Hands and a Clean Heart   pg. 19
Who may stand in his holy place? The one who has clean hands and a pure heart... Psalm 24:3b-4a

Lesson 4: The Word of God Brings Revival   pg. 29
Then Jesus declared, "I am the Bread of Life. He who comes to me will never go hungry, and he who believes in Me will never be thirsty" John 6:35

Lesson 5: How to Be a Fruity Christian   pg. 39
I am the vine; you are the branches. If you remain in me and I in you, you will bear much fruit; apart from me you can do nothing. John 15:5

Lesson 6: The Oil of Anointing   pg. 49
I can do all things through Christ who strengthens me. Philippians 4:13 (NKJV)

Lesson 7: Equipped by the Holy Spirit   pg. 57
For this reason, I remind you to fan into flame the gift of God, which is in you through the laying on of my hands. 2 Timothy 1:6

Lesson 8: PUSH – Pray Until Something Happens   pg. 63
Continue to ask, and God will give to you. Continue to search, and you will find. Continue to knock, and the door will open for you. Matthew 7:7 (ICB)

Lesson 9: Worship that Smells Good   pg. 71
God is Spirit, and those who worship Him must worship in spirit and truth. John 4:24 (NKJV)

Lesson 10: The Veil that Blocks Worship   pg. 77
Let us go right into the presence of God, with true hearts fully trusting him... Hebrews 10:22

Lesson 11: The Mercy Seat   pg. 83
The Lord is gracious and full of compassion, slow to anger and great in mercy. Psalm 145:8 (NKJV)

Lesson 12: The Glory of God   pg. 91
...Now, show me Your Glory. Exodus 33:18 NIV

Lesson 13: Into the Harvest Field   pg. 97
...Go into all the world and preach the good news to all creation. Luke 16:15

How To Use This Curriculum:

Scriptural Premise: God wants His people to enter His glory. From the very beginning creation, He has been drawing us into a closer relationship with Him. Children are not exempt from this call. In fact, God has always opened the door for children to enter His presence. That is why Jesus said, "From the lips of infants and children, You have ordained praise."

The Tabernacle of Moses is a blueprint for entering the glory of God. Each piece of furniture in the temple represents another aspect of our Christian lives. The pieces of furniture are listed below.

- Brazen Altar: Jesus is the sacrifice for our sin.
- Golden Laver: Jesus sanctifies us.
- Table of the Shewbread: Jesus is the Word of God that brings revival.
- The Golden Lampstand: The Holy Spirit brings fruit, anointing and the baptism of the Holy Spirit.
- The Table of Incense: God wants to fellowship with us through prayer and praise.
- The Veil: Jesus ripped the veil in two, destroying anything that blocks us from God's presence.
- The Mercy Seat: God, the father, is a merciful God and wants us to show His mercy.
- The Ark of the Covenant: God, the father, wants to show us His Glory.

Decorations: Decorations and set design should reflect a tabernacle. To create a backdrop, use the graphic of the Tabernacle included in digital downloads as a template. You can use any image included with this curriculum by projecting the image using a video projector onto a box or backdrop and drawing it.

You can also hang up curtains and make items to represent the tabernacle furniture. You will need the brazen altar (brass box with horns coming out of the four corners), golden laver (gold colored basin), table of showbread (table with 12 pieces of pita or unleavened bread), golden candlestick holder, table of incense (table with incense burning on it), veil, tall purple curtain, ark of the covenant with the mercy seat. If you decide to do this, I recommend having the ark on the backdrop with the 2 curtains for the veil opened so you can see the backdrop. Cardboard columns would also make a nice touch. Look at pictures online or the Tabernacle slide to get an idea how to place the furniture.

Use your creativity.

Italics: Italics are used for Scripture. They are also used in this curriculum for passages or speeches the teacher or worker may want to say in their own words. For skits, italics are only used to designate the person speaking.

Welcome:

Welcome: Each lesson will welcome the children with an introduction to that day's message.

Prayer: It's important to start each lesson with prayer.

Rules: A list of 5 Ups are included in the graphics available after registration. Rehearse the rules every week.

Theme Song: Get the kids up and moving at the beginning of every lesson with a fun theme song. Theme song that will work with this curriculum are *Glory Glory Glory* by the Rizers or *Glory to God Forever* by Fee. Depending on the church, you could also use *Every Hour* by Kayne West or *All Hail the Power of Jesus Name*.

Memory Verse: Every lesson has a memory verse. The verse will be included in a slide and will be illustrated in two ways. You can choose to use any of these illustrations to teach the verse, or you could use both throughout your lesson.

Memory Verse Talk: This is a short talk explaining what the verse means to the children. Memorizing God's Word is important, but it's more important for your students to know what a verse means.

Memory Verse Activity: Children learn by seeing, reading, hearing, and doing. The memory verse activity is a simple tool to help students remember the verse longer.

Game Time: A Game Time slide is included with registration for this curriculum. It isn't necessary to include a game with every week's lesson, but if you do, you should have a fun game that relates to the lessons. Game Time is the place for that. You may also want to save the game for last so, if the adult service runs long, you can play games until the parents arrive to retrieve their children.

Video Clips: *Building a Place for God's Glory Countdown* and video clips for some lessons are included with *Building a Place for God's Glory*. A link to download them will be sent through email after you have registered your curriculum. *Building Foundations* doesn't provide video curriculum to teach the lessons. Instead it provides short, fun video clips to help the children remember the lesson in a fun way.

Offering: Lessons include a short talk on why children should give in the offering. You can expand the fun by having an offering contest with the boys against the girls. You can use a scale with buckets or have two offering plates and count the money. Once a month or once a quarter, have a special reward for the winning team.

Praise & Worship: Each week, a time of praise and worship is included to ready the students' hearts to hear the Word of God. This curriculum does not provide music because every church has different musical needs.

Lesson of the Week:

Skit: A skit about each week's lesson is included. The skit uses Professor Confuzed, a live character skit with a confused professor who always gets everything wrong. Professor Confuzed can wear a lab coat or a shirt with a pocket protector. These skits require few props and only two people, the leader and another worker, making them easy for even small churches to use. Professor Confuzed is a live skit but could also be used with puppets, but it may need a few small modification when props are involved. During one lesson, a girl named Lucy is substituted for Professor Confuzed. A teenager or older child could easily play the part of Lucy.

Bible Story: Each week, a Bible story is included to go with the lesson.

Object Lessons: At least two object lessons illustrate the points of each week's lesson. Resources for the object lessons are not included.

Message: A short message ties up the lesson for the day and asks for a response from the students

Optional Resources: Optional Resources are needed with object lessons and other inactive events as suggestions for additional teaching activities. The props for optional resources are not included but are easy to obtain. Revival Fire for Kids also has downloadable resources to use for free with the purchase and registration of this curriculum.

Small Group Chat: Some children's ministries prefer to end each children's service with a small group chat or activity, or they have a small group Bible study at some time during the week. Small group chat questions are included for these purposes. Divide students into small groups of not more than six children. You can divide them by ages or include different ages together. Questions are included to help the leader facilitate a chat with the students about the lesson. Sometimes an activity or craft will also be included. Small group sessions will help your students go home with practical applications for what they have learned.

Home Application: Each lesson will include a handout for the children to take home. Each handout will include this week's memory verse, a summary of the lesson, and a Bible reading for each day. This handout is available as a printable PDF download upon registration of this curriculum. This will be helpful guide for parents who have family devotions.

Lesson 1: Prepare To Enter God's Presence

Focus Point: God wants us to prepare to enter His presence through thanksgiving, praise, and worship.

Goal: Children will learn to enter the presence of God through thanksgiving, praise & worship.

Memory Verse: Psalm 100:4 *Enter His gates with thanksgiving and His courts with praise; give thanks to Him and praise His name.*

Supplies Needed:

- Building a Place for God Videos (free with registration)
- Building a Place for God Jpeg Slides (free with registration)
- copies of Building a Place for God Family Devotional Sheet
- Professor Confuzed costume: lab coat or a shirt with a pocket protector
- 2 hats
- 2 scarves
- 2 pairs of large boots or overshoes
- 2 jackets
- 2 umbrellas
- picture of Queen Elizabeth
- index cards
- scotch tape
- swim goggles or another toy you would take in the pool
- one notebook or journal for each child

Opening: *Building a Place for God's Glory Countdown* or *Building a Place for God's Glory* Intro Slide (Available free with registration of this curriculum.)

Welcome: Welcome the children and tell them how happy you are to see them. If you have a smaller church, this is the time how their week has been and ask for prayer requests.

Good morning. Did any of you prepare to come to church today? I'll bet most of you did. Raise your hand if you prepared to come to church in any of these ways.

- *For instance, did any of you set an alarm clock to wake up on time?*
- *How many of you brushed your teeth before you came?*
- *Did any of you take a shower or a bath?*
- *Did any of you put on your church clothes instead of coming in what you slept in?*

It looks like we all prepared to come to church. Now we are going to learn how to prepare to enter the presence of God.

Prayer: Ask a child to pray over the service.

Rules: (use rules slide)

Go over the *5 Ups Rules*: 1. Sit up straight. 2. Listen up. 3. Hush up. 4. Don't get up and run around or go to the bathroom. 5. Worship Up! (stand and participate during praise and worship)

Theme or Activity Songs: Choose one or two fast moving activity songs that goes with the curriculum.

Game Time: Preparing for Bad Weather (use game time slide)

Supplies needed: 2 hats, 2 scarves, 2 pairs of large boots or overshoes, 2 jackets, 2 umbrellas

There are a lot of things we prepare for. Can you name a few? Have the children name some things we need to prepare for. Suggest preparing for the weather, if nobody else mentions it.

Divide all of the children into two teams to dress one person from each team. Each clothing item is passed to everyone on the team it belongs to before being put on the person. The team who dresses their person for the weather first, with an open umbrella, wins.

It's important to be prepared for bad weather. It's even more important to prepare to enter the presence of God.

Memory Verse: Psalm 100:4 *Enter His gates with thanksgiving and His courts with praise; give thanks to Him and praise His name.*

Memory Verse Talk: (use Building a Place for God's Glory lesson 1, slide A)

Supplies needed: picture of Queen Elizabeth

I read a book once that was all about the queen of England. Did you know that the Queen has knights?

Once a year the palace sends out invitations to invite people to the royal ceremony to dub knights. That means to make people knights. You can only come if you get an invitation. I've never gotten an invitation, but I hope I will someday. The guests arrive the day before the event. Each person who is supposed to be knighted has to be shown exactly how to behave.

They have to kneel on one knee on a special stool before the queen. Then the queen takes a sword and taps it on their shoulders. It doesn't hurt though. She does it lightly. Then when the Queen shakes their hand, they are supposed to leave. These special rules teach you how to act in government ceremonies are called protocol. Everyone has to follow protocol when they meet the queen. They can't just run up and say Howdy.

I was thinking, if we show that much respect to the queen of England, Shouldn't we show God, the King of Kings, respect too? Psalm 100:4 says Enter His gates with thanksgiving and His courts with praise; give thanks to Him and praise His name. I guess you would call that Heavenly Protocol.

Memory Verse Activity: Entering with Thanksgiving

Supplies needed: index cards with each word of the memory verse on it, scotch tape

We are going to enter God's gate and courts while we do the memory verse. Each of you take a card with a word from the memory verse on it.

If there are too many children, they can break into teams for each word.

When it is your turn (or your team's turn), *place your word on the wall or board, first you have to think of something to praise or thank God for.* (For teams, each member of the team must think of something.)

After the children tape all the words of the verse on the wall or board in order, have them say the verse together.

Offering: Giving Because We Love God

Tell about a famous singer or actor who charges people to meet them for autographs or pictures. *Aren't you glad you don't have to pay an offering to meet with God? God wants us to give generously, but He wants to meet with us right where we are. We give because we love God.*

Skit: Prepared for Fishing

Some of these skits are long. If you like, you can adlib making sure you convey the main point of the skit.

Supplies Needed: Professor costume

Professor Confuzed: (enters) Hello everyone. I am Professor Confuzed. It is so good to see you.

Leader: Well, hello, Professor Confuzed. It is so good to see you too. I'm so glad you could come to visit today. So, what have you been up to?

Professor: I have taken a long journey. It took me many months to complete this journey and come to Akron (Chose your city) to be with you here today.

Leader: Wow, Professor, you must have traveled to some place a long way from here.

Professor: Yes, it has been a long journey.

Leader: Where did you go?

Professor: Cleveland. (Chose a large city close to you.)

Leader: Do you mean Cleveland, Tennessee? (Chose another state with the same city.)

Professor: No, Cleveland, Ohio.

Leader: But, Professor, it doesn't take months to go from Cleveland to Akron. It takes about an hour and a half.

Professor: I don't understand. I have been traveling for months. I saw a lot of wonderful sites though.

The Grand Canyon was beautiful. (If you live in Arizona or a nearby state, chose a location across the country such as Niagara Falls.)

Leader: Professor, the Grand Canyon is in Arizona. You don't go to Arizona on your way to Akron.

Professor: You don't? I must have made a wrong turn.

Leader: Oh, Professor, you're so confused. What are you planning to do now?

Professor: I'm going fishing and camping with some friends of mine.

Leader: When are you leaving?

Professor: In ten minutes.

Leader: Where's all your stuff?

Professor: What stuff?

Leader: Your camping and fishing equipment.

Professor: I need equipment?

Leader: When you go on a fishing trip you need to prepare by taking along things that you need.

Professor: I don't understand. I thought that all I had to do is go to a camping spot by a lake.

Leader: You have to prepare first. For instance, Professor, what are you going to fish with?

Professor: I don't know. I guess I can stick my hands in the lake and pull out the fish.

Leader: I'm afraid that doesn't work very well. That's why most people take along a fishing pole when they plan to go fishing.

Professor: Amazing.

Leader: Professor, where do you plan to sleep?

Professor: I thought I could sleep in a tree like Tarzan.

Leader: That's one possibility, but aren't you afraid that you might fall out of the tree?

Professor: I never thought of that. What do you suggest I do?

Leader: Most people prepare for where they are going to sleep by taking along a tent and a sleeping bag to sleep in.

Professor: That's absolutely amazing. I never thought of that. Tell me more.

Leader: Well, Professor, there is something else to consider. Are you going to eat the fish you catch raw or are you planning on cooking them?

Professor: I hate raw fish. I'm going to cook them.

Leader: What are you going to light the fire with?

Professor: I don't know. I could rub two sticks together.

Leader: It's hard to start a fire that way. Most people use matches.

Professor: That's incredible.

Leader: You'll also need a pan to cook the fish in, a knife to cut up and clean the fish and a fork and plate to eat the fish with.

Professor: I guess I need to prepare some more before I go on this fishing trip.

Leader: Yes Professor, I believe your right.

Professor: I'd better go now. I need to buy the sticks to start the fire with.

Leader: Oh Professor, you're so confused. Kids, some people plan and prepare to do just about everything, but when it comes to entering into the presence of God, they are just as confused as the professor. They think they can go into the presence of God without spending any time thanking, praising or worshipping Him. Just as you need to prepare to go camping or fishing, it's even more important to prepare to meet with God.

Bible Story: Walking, and Leaping, and Praising God (Acts 3:1-10)

All of the children can participate in this story. Have them do these motions for the following words.

Alms: rub fingers together and say "show me the money"
Walking/walk: walk 2 steps
Leaping: jump up and down
Praising God: Shout halleluiah

Have the students practice the motions a few times. Read the story from Acts 3:1-10 in New King James Version and have the student do the motions.

When the lame man was healed, he spent time thanking a praising God for what he had received. Because of that, other people came to know about God. Imagine how God could use our lives if we spent time thanking, praising, and worshipping Him for all he has done for us.

Praise Break: Psalm 100 (use Building a Place for God's Glory lesson 1 praise slide)

Have the children read Psalm 100 with you. Encourage them to read it again while they praise God. Have a short testimony time, and encourage the students to name what they are thankful for.

Shout for joy to the Lord, all the earth.

Worship the Lord with gladness; come before him with joyful songs.

Know that the Lord is God. It is he who made us, and we are his; we are his people, the sheep of his pasture.

Enter his gates with thanksgiving and his courts with praise; give thanks to him and praise his name.

For the Lord is good and his love endures forever; his faithfulness continues through all generations.

Praise and Worship: Choose a couple of fast song and a slow song to lead children into praise and worship. It works well to talk to the children about what worship is and why it's important before you enter into this time. You can have a children's praise team, but until they understand leading praise and worship, have an adult leader or yourself be the worship leader.

Object Lessons:

1. How Deep Do You Want To Go (Ezekiel 47:1-5)

Supplies Needed: Swim goggles or another toy you would take in the pool

How many of you have ever been swimming? Some children are a little afraid of the water when they first go swimming. Some children are so afraid that they will only wade in up to their ankles. Most children, though, after a while will get a little braver and wade in to their knees. Some children will even go to their waists. How many of you have ever been in water deeper than your waist? How many of you have ever been in water as deep as your neck? Some children aren't afraid of the water at all because they have been swimming a long time and they will even jump in water way over their head. How many of you children have ever done that? The same is true spiritually.

The prophet, Ezekiel had a vision once about a river that flowed from the throne of God. The river represented the presence of God. An angel told Ezekiel to go into the river about one third of a mile. When Ezekiel did the water came to his ankles. This represents children who accept Jesus as their Savior, but they never really go any further in their relationship with God.

The angel again spoke to Ezekiel and told him to go in another third of a mile. When Ezekiel did, the water was up to his knees. This is where children are who have accepted Jesus as their savior and start coming to church pretty regularly. Sometimes they even pray and thank God for saving them. But that's all the further they ever go.

The angel then told Ezekiel to go into the river another third of a mile. At this point, the water came to Ezekiel's waist. This represents children are who have gone a little further in their relationship with God. They go to church whenever they can. While they are at church, they listen to the Word of God being taught and preached and they try to obey the Bible. They pray and during worship time at church, they will even raise their hands and praise God out loud. They love God and they love to praise Him, but there is still something missing.

The angel of the Lord told Ezekiel to go out into the water another third of a mile. When Ezekiel did

this, the river became so deep and mighty that Ezekiel could not even swim in it. The only thing Ezekiel could do is surrender and go with the flow of the river. This is the true worship that God wants for His children. He wants you to completely surrender to Him and let Him take control. When you do that God will take you into His Glory.

2. The Tabernacle

(Use Building a Place for God's Glory lesson 1, slides B, C, and D)

(Show slide B) *The Tabernacle of Moses was a very important place in Bible times. God had Moses build the Tabernacle so that God would have a place on Earth for people to go to be with God. In was a place for God's Glory to live Today, we don't have to go to a tabernacle to enter the presence of God because we become the temple of God when we are saved. God is building a Tabernacle in our hearts where He can live.*

In the Tabernacle, there were three areas. You would enter the first area called the outer court through a gate. When we are grateful and thankful to God for what He has done for us, in our hearts, we are entering through His gate. Take some time to have the children thank God.

(Show slide C) *Inside the Tabernacle was a building. It had two areas. The first area was called the Inner Courts or the Holy Place. That's where God's presence was. Very few people could go into the Holy Place. We go in the Inner Courts when we praise God. Even though every Christian can now go into the Holy Place, most don't take time to praise God. Let's take a moment to praise Him.* You can encourage the children to shout Halleluiah or Praise the Lord if they are new to this or need direction.

(Show slide D) *The second part of the building was the Holy of Holies. Only one person could go into the Holy of Holies and he could only go in once a year. The Holy of Holies was a place built for God's Glory to live. It was where God showed man His Glory in olden days. Now every Christian can enter God's presence any time they want through praising and worshipping Him. When you surrender or yield everything to God and worship Him, He will show us His Glory.*

Have you ever wondered what it means in the Bible when it says to enter God's gates or His courts? It's not like there's a special place we can go where there's a big gate we can enter, but there used to be. In Bible times, God wanted His people to build a tabernacle where they could worship Him. He wanted them to thank Him when they entered the gate into the tabernacle and praise Him as they went into the court or the area of the tabernacle. We don't need a tabernacle now because we are now the temple of God. Whenever we want to enter the presence of God, we can do so with a spirit of thanksgiving, praise, and worship. God wants us to spend time with Him.

When we worship God with our whole heart, soul, mind, and strength, we prepare to enter God's Glory. Let's spend some time worshipping God.

You may want to have the children find a place to kneel or lay on the floor while you place worship music. Encourage them to worship God with everything in them. That means they might laugh or cry or just soak in God's peace. Don't limit God on how He wants to move in them.

Message: True Worship

In Romans 12:1, Scripture tells us what true worship is. Therefore, I urge you, brothers and sisters, in view of God's mercy, to offer your bodies as a living sacrifice, holy and pleasing to God—this is your true and proper worship. What this means is that true worship comes from giving God ourselves. We have been spending time during this lesson praising and worshipping God. Now it is time to surrender ourselves to God.

For response time today, have children continue worshipping at the altar. As they worship, allow God to lead you and pray for each child. You don't have to pray a long prayer or say anything at all. Lay you hand on each child's head, and wait for God to do what He wills. Make sure you have catchers who firmly place their hands on students' backs and ease them down if they fall. God may move in many ways that might be unusual. Expect God to move, and prepare for it.

Small Group Chat:

Supplies needed: one notebook or journal for each child

For this small group chat, take some time to talk to your students about what happened during response time and how God is moving in their lives. Give them each a notebook to write or draw pictures of what God is showing them during this teaching series. Encourage them to bring their notebooks and Bibles to church every week.

If some of your students don't have Bibles, this might be a good time to provide Bibles for them.

Building a Place for God's Glory Lesson 1

Prepare to Enter God's Presence Family Devotions Handout

Memory Verse: Psalm 100:4 *Enter His gates with thanksgiving and His courts with praise; give thanks to Him and praise His name.*

Summary: Sometimes, we believe we could never really enter God's presence. The truth is every Christian can enter the presence of God.

This sheet is provided to help families with devotions to go with the lessons your children learned in children's church this week. Included is a daily Bible reading to use for discussions.

Monday: Read Psalm 100. This chapter tells how we enter God's presence: through shouts of joy, worshiping with gladness, thanksgiving, and praise.

Tuesday: Read Acts 3:1-10. When the lame man at the temple was healed, he went around leaping and praising God. We have so much to praise God for. Maybe we should spend time jumping up and down and praising God.

Wednesday: Read Ezekiel 47:1-5. How deep do we want to go with God?

Thursday: Read Luke 10:27. How do we show our love for God with our hearts? Our souls? Our strength? Our minds?

Friday: Read Romans 12:1. How can we become living sacrifices to God?

Saturday: Read 1 Chronicles 16:34. Talk about all the things we should thank God for.

Family Activity: Thanksgiving Chain

Supplies needed: scissors, stickers, pencils, crayons, glue and construction paper

Create a construction paper chain by doing the following. Have each person in the family draw pictures or write what they are thankful for on a strip of construction paper. Do this multiple times. Have each person name what they are thankful for as they connect their strips to the chain.

Lesson 2: The Fire That Forgives

Focus Point: Jesus died so that our sins could be forgiven. He is the sacrifice that was put on the Brazen Altar

Goal: Children will ask God to forgive them of any sin, pride, or unforgiveness. If not saved, they will ask Jesus to be their savior.

Memory Verse: *Repent therefore and be converted, that your sins may be blotted out, so that times of refreshing may come from the presence of the Lord* Acts 3:19 (NKJV)

Supplies Needed:

- Building a Place for God Videos (free with registration)
- Building a Place for God Jpeg Slides (free with registration)
- copies of Building a Place for God Family Devotional Sheet
- Professor Confuzed costume: lab coat or a shirt with a pocket protector
- beach balls or playground balls
- picture of a jellyfish
- chalk or marker boars
- eraser
- cardboard or wooden box painted to resemble the brazen altar
- 4 pieces of flash paper

Opening: *Building a Place for God's Glory Countdown* or *Building a Place for God's Glory* Intro Slide (Available free with registration of this curriculum.)

Welcome: *Today, we are going to talk about fire, but not just any fire. We are talking about the fire of God. The fire of God doesn't burn things up like regular fire. Instead it cleans our hearts and forgives our sins.*

Prayer: Ask a child to pray over the service.

Rules: (use rules slide)

Go over the *5 Ups Rules*: 1. Sit up straight. 2. Listen up. 3. Hush up. 4. Don't get up and run around or go to the bathroom. 5. Worship Up! (stand and participate during praise and worship)

Theme or Activity Songs: Choose one or two fast moving activity songs that goes with the curriculum.

Game Time: Get Rid of Sin (Use Game Time slide)

Supplies needed: 3 – 5 beach balls or playground balls (You could also use balloons)

It's very important in our Christian life to get rid of the sin that sometimes creeps in. That's why it is important to allow the fire of God to forgive us and cleanse us.

Form two teams, one on each side of the room. Explain to the children that they want to try to keep the balls on the other side of the room. The balls represent sins. They must stay at their seats and try to hit the balls to the other side. Have spotters to throw the balls back in so that children don't have to leave their seats. Play music during the game. When the music stops, the team with the least number of balls wins.

Offering: Blessed Through Tithing

God wants to bless His people. He does that in many ways, but He also wants us to show everything we have belongs to God. The way we do that is by tithing. Tithing is giving the first 10% of everything we earn or are given to God. We do that by giving the tithe in church offerings. 10% is easy to figure out or you can ask an adult. 10% of every dollar is 10 cents. 10 % of every ten dollars is one dollar. Let's decide to begin tithing today.

This is a good time to answer any questions your students might have about tithing.

Memory Verse: *Repent therefore and be converted, that your sins may be blotted out, so that times of refreshing may come from the presence of the Lord* Acts 3:19 (NKJV)

Memory Verse Talk: (use Building a Place for God's Glory lesson 2, slide A)

Supplies needed: picture of an Alatina Alata jellyfish or Building a Place for God's Glory lesson 1, slide B

(Show picture or slide B) *This is a picture of a jellyfish. There are many kinds of jellyfish in the ocean, but they all sting. Most jellyfish give minor stings that can be treated at home. They are a lot like bee stings. There are some jellyfish that have much worse stings. Some will put you in the hospital. They can hurt you very badly or even kill you.*

This jellyfish is very pretty. It is called an Alatina Alata, but it is sometimes called a sea wasp because its sting hurts so bad. Its sting can not only send you to the hospital, sometimes it can kill you. You never want to be stung by an Alatina Alata.

Sin is a lot like the Alatina Alata. It looks pretty sometimes, but it can hurt you really bad. What make it worse is that anyone with sin in his or her life can't enter God's presence. That's why Jesus died for our sins, so we could go into the presence of God.

We've all done wrong things and sinned against God, but the Bible has a solution in Acts 3:19 "Repent therefore and be converted, that your sins may be blotted out, so that times of refreshing may come from the presence of the Lord."

That means if we do sin, we should ask God to forgive us, and He'll forgive us and refresh us in His presence.

Memory Verse Activity: Memory Verse Bounce

Supplies needed: one of the balls from game time.

Form the children into a large circle. Have them pass the ball to each other. When a student has the ball, he should say the next word of the memory verse. Continue playing until they've said the entire verse a number of times.

Skit: Professor Confuzed Learns About Fire

Supplies needed: Professor Confuzed costume

Professor Confuzed: Hello everybody. I'm back.

Leader: Well, hello, Professor Confuzed. I'm glad you decided to come and visit us again this week.

Professor: Yes, I came for a very important reason.

Leader: Really? What reason is that?

Professor: I heard you were talking about fire today, and I have been studying fire. So, I thought I might be of some assistance.

Leader: Well, Professor, we are not just talking about any fire. We are talking about the fire of God.

Professor: Fire is fire. It's all the same.

Leader: Not exactly, but go ahead, Professor Confuzed. Tell us what you have learned about fire.

Professor: I have learned that fire on the inside of the house is okay, and fire on the outside of the house is not.

Leader: Professor, fire can be dangerous on the inside of the house and on the outside of the house.

Professor: I don't understand. People use fire on their gas stoves to cook, and they have fire in their gas furnaces. I've even seen people who have places they burn fires in their living rooms called fireplaces, but when I see a fire on the outside of a house, the fire trucks are always trying to put the fire out.

Leader: Professor, fire is always dangerous. Fire in stoves, furnaces, and fireplaces are contained so that they won't burn anything down. You should never play with fire because you can't control it. The fire you saw on the outside of the house was dangerous because it wasn't contained. It was dangerous because it was out of control.

Professor: Hmmm, very interesting. I will have to study a little more, but I have noticed something else. Fire is very cold.

Leader: Cold? Professor, you are confused. What makes you think fire is cold?

Professor: I read it in the Bible.

Leader: In the Bible?

Professor: Yes, that's right. Haven't you ever read about Moses and the burning bush?

Leader: Yes, but how does that prove fire is cold?

Professor: Moses saw the burning bush, but the bush never burnt up. It was not consumed. If a burning bush doesn't burn up, it must be because fire is cold.

Leader: Professor, you're confusing man's fire with God's fire. Man's fire is very hot. Although it can do some very helpful things when it is under control, man's fire is dangerous. When it is not under control, it can be very destructive. God's fire is a spiritual fire. It only destroys sin in our lives. It's meant to forgive us and remove our sin and give us times of refreshing in God's presence. It doesn't want to harm us.

Professor: So, God's fire is under control.

Leader: Nobody can control the fire of God. The Bible says God is a consuming fire.

Professor: Then how do we control God's fire so that it is not dangerous?

Leader: We don't. God wants us to surrender to Him so that He can have control

Professor: That's amazing. Well I have to hurry and get home right away.

Leader: Why, Professor. What's wrong?

Professor: I thought that fire didn't hurt anything if it was inside a house, so I built a fire in my living room.

Leader: It's all right, Professor. Lots of people have fires in their fireplaces.

Professor: That's true, but I don't have a fireplace. I hope the house didn't burn down.

Leader: Oh Professor, you're so confused. I hope your house is all right. Good-bye, Professor Confuzed.

Kids, some people never are forgiven of their sins only because they never give their lives to God so that He can forgive them and have control of their lives. That's sad because that is the only way we can have a relationship with God.

Bible Story: Isaiah Sees God (Isaiah 6)

(Use Building a Place for God's Glory lesson 1, slides C, D, and lesson 2 praise slide)

Tell the story found Isaiah chapter 6 in your own words using the slides provided.

In Isaiah 6, the Bible talks about when the prophet Isaiah saw the Lord. His friend, the king, had just died. He'd gone to the temple to pray about it. Sometimes when we are sad or going through a hard

time, God will show Himself to us. That's what happened to Isaiah.

(Show Slide C) Suddenly Isaiah saw the Lord right in front of him. The Bible says the Lord was high and exalted, seated on a throne, and had a robe that filled the temple.

(Show slide D) That would be amazing, but that's not all he saw. He saw angels with six wings each. Two wings covered their faces. Two wings covered their feet. They were using the last two wings to fly.

(Show Lesson 2 praise slide) Then the angels started shouting, "Holy, holy, holy is the Lord Almighty; the whole earth is full of his glory." When they did that, the temple shook and was filled with smoke.

What would you do if you saw something like that appear before you? I'll tell you what Isaiah did. He cried. He knew he had sinned, and sin can't be in the presence of God. He cried, "I am ruined! For I am a man of unclean lips, and I live among a people of unclean lips, and my eyes have seen the King, the Lord Almighty."

Isaiah repented of his sin. When he did, God had an angel touch his lips with a coal from the fire. Coal taken from the fire would usually burn, but this was God's fire. It took away his sin. Today we can be cleansed of our sins by asking Jesus to forgive us. When we do, He takes the blood that He shed on the cross and cleanses us from our sins so that we can see God.

Praise Break (Use Building a Place for God's Glory lesson 2 praise slide)

Let's praise God using the words the angels sang.

Have the children repeat the words on the slide. Isaiah 6:3 ... *Holy, holy, holy, is the LORD of hosts: the whole earth is full of His glory.*

After they repeated it a few times, have them give testimonies about times they felt God's presence. If your students aren't ready for this, give a testimony of your own.

Praise and Worship: Choose a couple of fast song and a slow song to lead children into praise and worship. It works well to talk to the children about what worship is and why it's important before you enter into this time. You can have a children's praise team, but until they understand leading praise and worship, have an adult leader or yourself be the worship leader.

Object Lessons:

1. The Big Eraser

Supplies needed: chalk or marker board with different kinds of sins on it, eraser

Have you ever done a math problem on a marker board? The cool thing about it is when you mess up, you can erase it and do it over. Wouldn't it be awesome if we could do "do overs" in life. Erase the sins and write the word Jesus in large letters. *When Jesus forgives us of our sins, it's like having a do over.*

2. The Brazen Altar

(Use Building a Place for God's Glory lesson 2, slide E)

Supplies needed: paint a cardboard or wooden box to resemble the brazen altar or use slide E, 4 pieces of flash paper (Flash paper burns quickly and can be purchased online or at magic shops. You can also visit YouTube to find out how to make your own flash paper.)

Use four pieces of flash paper with the different offerings written on them: sin, our lives, our time and talents, peace. The paper burns very quickly, and you may want to practice with it before using it with the students.

(Show Building a Place for God's Glory lesson 2, slide E or wooden box) *When the tabernacle in Bible days was first entered, everyone would have to go to the brazen altar before they could go in further. The brazen altar was the place where animals were sacrificed to pay for sin. The fire on the altar was constantly burning.*

There were different kinds of sacrifices given at the brazen altar. Each shows how we want to enter into the presence of God.

For each offering, show the corresponding piece of flash paper. After talking about each sacrifice, light the paper on fire.

Sin and Trespass Offerings: Jesus was our sin offering. We shouldn't sin, but when we do, we can ask God to forgive us and erase the sin.

Burnt Offering: When we are saved, we give our lives and our own self-interests to God. We surrender our lives to Him, but this shouldn't only be a one-time thing. We should continually offer our lives to God.

Meal Offering: When we offer our lives to God, we also offer our time and our talents so God can use us in the Kingdom of God. We each have a purpose, and God wants us to give our time and talents to Him so He can use us in that purpose.

Peace Offering: God wants us to forgive others just as He forgave us. If we have anything against someone, the Bible tells us to get it right before we worship. God wants us to make peace with others.

Today we don't have to sacrifice animals at the brazen altar, because Jesus sacrificed Himself on the cross for our sins. We accept His sacrifice repenting and surrendering our lives to Him.

Message: Times of Refreshing

When we repent and our sins are blotted out, today's memory verse promises times of refreshing in the presence of God. Sometimes we hear promises like that, but we don't understand what they mean.

Refresh means to revive or renew. So, when we spend time in the presence of God, revival and renewal in our spirits is assure. To spend time in the presence of God, first we have to confess our sins to God and ask Him to blot them out.

Encourage the students to find a quiet place to pray and repent of any sins they may have committed. They may need forgiveness for pride or unforgiveness or they might want to commit their time and talents to the Lord.

For those who have never asked God to be their Savior, you may want to ask them to come aside with you to pray the sinner's prayer. For those who may not know of any sins they have committed, suggest they ask God if there is anything they need to confess. Afterwards, have them return to their seats.

Now that we have repented and had our sins blotted out, it is time for the times of refreshing in the presence of the Lord. As we spend time worshipping God, He may give us times of refreshing in various ways. Some might be filled with the Holy Spirit and begin to speak in other tongues. Some might be filled with joy and begin to laugh. Some might have peace sweep over them. Some might be healed of hurts and begin to cry. Whatever God decides to do, yield to Him as he refreshes you.

Spend time worshipping God. Don't rush this. Give God room to move. When you feel led by the Holy Spirit, place your hand on each child and wait for God.

Small Group Chat:

Encourage the students to talk about what happened today at the altar. Have them write down their experience in their journals.

Building a Place for God's Glory Lesson 2

The Fire that Forgives Family Devotions Handout

Memory Verse: Acts 3:19 (NKJV) *Repent therefore and be converted, that your sins may be blotted out, so that times of refreshing may come from the presence of the Lord*

Summary: Most Christians look forward to times of refreshing and revival in the presence of the Lord. These times come only after repentance and forgiveness of sins.

This sheet is provided to help families with devotions to go with the lessons your children learned in children's church this week. Included is a daily Bible reading to use for discussions.

Monday: Read Matthew 3:11. This verse talks about God baptizing us in His Spirit and fire. Fire can be scary to kids, but this kind of fire is God's cleansing fire that causes us to step into His presence.

Tuesday: Read Isaiah 6:1-6. When the Prophet Isaiah saw the Lord and how holy He is, he was overcome because of his sin. God cleansed Him just as God cleanses us from sin today.

Wednesday: Read 1 John 1:9. When we sin, we need to confess our sins, and God will forgive us.

Thursday: Read Isaiah 43:25. God will blot out our sins like an eraser on a marker board. He promises never to remember them again.

Friday: Read Proverbs 28:13. God doesn't want us to hide our sins. He wants us to confess them and turn from them so we can be blessed.

Saturday: Read Psalm 103:8-22. God's love and compassion removes our sins as far as the east is from the west. The east and west never meet.

Family Activity: The Repent Game

Supplies needed: Look up The Repent Game on Kirk Cameron's Website at this link.
http://kirkcameron.com/articles/the-repent-game

Play the repent game with your children. A variation of this game could be to play Hide and Seek. Children hide while you count to ten. When you are finished, shout, "I love you. Repent." Children leave their hiding places and run to you. The first child to reach the parent wins.

Lesson 3: Clean Hands and a Pure Heart

Focus Point: Jesus wants to sanctify and cleanse us. He is our golden laver.

Goal: Children will ask God to search their hearts and cleanse them of anything wrong in them.

Memory Verse: *Who may stand in his holy place? The one who has clean hands and a pure heart...* Psalm 24:3b-4a

Supplies Needed:

- Building a Place for God Videos (free with registration)
- Building a Place for God Jpeg Slides (free with registration)
- copies of Building a Place for God Family Devotional Sheet
- Professor Confuzed costume: lab coat or a shirt with a pocket protector
- 2 washcloths
- 2 towels
- 2 bars of soap
- 2 bowls of water
- china cup
- old mug
- a large basin of water
- clean towels

Opening: *Building a Place for God's Glory Countdown* or *Building a Place for God's Glory* Intro Slide (Available free with registration of this curriculum.)

Welcome: *How many of you took a bath last night or this morning or got washed up before coming to church? Today we're going to talk about having a clean heart. Of course, you can't open yourself up and wash your heart with soap and water, but if you ask Jesus, He will remove everything that displeases Him out of your heart and make it clean and pure.*

Prayer: Ask a child to pray over the service.

Rules: (use rules slide)

Go over the *5 Ups Rules*: 1. Sit up straight. 2. Listen up. 3. Hush up. 4. Don't get up and run around or go to the bathroom. 5. Worship Up! (stand and participate during praise and worship)

Theme or Activity Songs: Choose one or two fast moving activity songs that goes with the curriculum.

Game Time: Washing Up (use game time slide)

Supplies needed: 2 washcloths, 2 towels, 2 bars of soap, 2 bowls of water

It's very important in our Christian life to ask God to cleanse us when we do something wrong just as it is important to wash up every day.

Assign two teams. Pick one child from each team. Have that child leave the room for a moment. Hide the washcloths, towels and bars of soap. Let the children know they may not tell their teammate where these items are, but they can yell cold, warm, warmer, hot, etc. When the two children come back in, explain to them that they need to wash their hands.

They must each find one washcloth, one towel and one bar of soap. Explain how their teammates will help them. Once they have found one of each of the items, they must run to the bowl of water, wash their hands with soap and dry them with the towel. The child who finishes washes his or her hands first wins.

Offering: Deciding What to Give

Read 2 Corinthians 9:7 to the students. *Each of you should give what you have decided in your heart to give, not reluctantly or under compulsion, for God loves a cheerful giver.*

God cares more about our motives when we give then how much we give. He wants us to give because we love God and we have decided to give, not because someone forces us to give. He wants us to be happy when we give.

As we give in this offering, I want you all to show how happy you are to give. You can clap or cheer or even laugh. God loves a cheerful giver.

Memory Verse: *Who may stand in his holy place? The one who has clean hands and a pure heart...* Psalm 24:3b-4a

Memory Verse Talk: (Use Building a Place for God's Glory Lesson 3 Slide A)

God wants us to come into His Holy Place. That doesn't only mean Heaven. On Earth, God's Holy Place is a place of joy, peace, and love where we know Him in a greater way. There are only two requirements for coming into His Holy Place: clean hands and a pure heart. Clean hands means doing the right things, and a pure heart means doing them for the right reasons. Nobody has clean hands and a pure heart on their own, but Jesus does. When we surrender to Him, He washes our hands and purifies our hearts so we can come into His Holy Place. We can't do it on our own. He is the One who makes us Holy.

Memory Verse Activity: Clean Hands Pure Heart

Have the students stand and say the verse out loud if they meet the conditions you call out. Here are some examples:

- Brown eyes
- Blue hair
- Wearing red
- Brushed teeth today
- Took a shower or a bath this morning
- Ate breakfast
- Went to school last week

End the activity with the following: Clean Hands, Pure Heart

Whether the students stand or not, let them know they can only have clean hands and a pure heart through Jesus.

Skit: Professor Confuzed Takes a Bath

Supplies needed: Professor Confuzed costume

Professor: Hello.

Leader: Well, hello, Professor. It's nice to see you again.

Professor: It's nice to see you again too. (Leader reaches up to shake Professor Confuzed's hand.) Don't shake my hand.

Leader: What? I don't understand.

Professor: I said, please don't shake my hand.

Leader: Why don't you want me to shake your hand, Professor? Are you confused?

Professor: Of course, I'm not confused. I just don't want to take another bath. I've already taken 12 baths today, and my skin is starting to shrivel.

Leader: Now, I'm confused.

Professor: And you always say that I'm the one who's always confused.

Leader: Professor, why did you take 12 baths today?

Professor: I have been studying about germs. Do you know that most colds and virus start from touching something that someone with a cold has touched or from shaking someone's hand?

Leader: Now I understand why you didn't want to shake my hand, but why did you take 12 baths?

Professor: To get the germs washed off of my hands, of course. And you say I'm confused.

Leader: Ah Professor, you are the one who's confused. You don't need to take and entire bath every time you touch something.

Professor: Yes, I do. I just told you how colds start with hand contact. The best way to avoid colds is to keep your hands clean.

Leader: That's true, but you still don't need to take an entire bath every time you touch something. You can wash just your hands.

Professor: Wash my hands? I'm confused.

Leader: When your hands are dirty, you only need to wash your hands. You don't need to wash everything. If you want, you can even buy antibacterial hand soap to fight germs.

Professor: That's amazing. That means I only have to take a bath once a year. I just have to wash my hands every time I touch something.

Leader: Professor, I still think you're a little confused. You need to take a bath more than once a year, but you don't have to take one when only your hands are dirty.

Professor: Thank-you for that valuable information. Now that I'm not taking so many baths, I can work more on my new project.

Leader: What new project?

Professor: I'm trying to find out why the water drains out of the bathtub if you don't use the bathtub stopper. I have a lot of work to do. Good-bye.

A lot of Christians are as confused as Professor Confuzed about what it takes to be clean before God. They think that every time you fail, you must be saved again. The truth is God wants to give us a clean and pure heart. We need to ask God to show us where our hearts are not clean. and He will cleanse us in those areas.

Bible Story: David's Disaster (2 Samuel 11-12)

God only allows those with a pure heart to enter His presence – people like King David. In Acts 13:22, the Lord said, "I have found David, son of Jesse, a man after my own heart; he will do everything I want him to do." David proved his love for God by obeying the Lord.

When he was a boy, David was a faithful shepherd to his sheep. He even fought off a lion and a bear. Ask the children if this pleased God.

When no one else had the courage to face the giant Goliath, David did not back down because he trusted the Lord. Ask the children if this pleased God.

When David was running from King Saul to protect his life, David did not murder Saul even though he had the opportunity. Ask the children if this pleased God.

When David became the king of Israel, he showed great kindness to Saul's crippled grandson. Ask the children if this pleased God.

One day while King David was at the palace, he saw a beautiful woman named Bathsheba who lived nearby. Bathsheba's husband was away serving with the army, so David decided to bring Bathsheba to the palace. Then he made sure her husband was on the front lines so he wouldn't make it back from the war. Ask the children if this pleased God. You may have to encourage the students to say no because they've been in the habit of saying yes.

David knew it was wrong, but he still did it. When he was finally confronted with his sin, he confessed, "I have sinned against the Lord." (2 Samuel 12:13). David prayed in Psalm 51:10, "Create in me a pure heart, O God: and renew a steadfast spirit within me."

David confessed his sin and repented to God. Ask the children if this pleased God.

God took David's sin and forgave him. It doesn't matter how bad we sin, when we confess to God and ask the Lord to create a pure heart in us, He will do it.

Skit: Professor Confuzed is Upset With God

Professor Confuzed: I'm really confused now. I just can't believe it.

Leader: You can't believe what.

Professor: That God would make a mistake like that!

Leader: God make a mistake? What are you talking about?

Professor: You are the one that just told everyone here about it.

Leader: I didn't say God made a mistake. I only explained how God forgave David.

Professor: Yep! That's what I'm confused about.

Leader: I don't understand.

Professor: David committed some BIG sins: taking another man's wife and making sure her husband never returned from the war. And God forgave David, just like that!

Leader: But isn't that good news?

Professor: It's not fair! Why should David have gotten away with it? If I were God, I would have made David go live in Antarctica without any shoes. Or maybe have made the king move into a doghouse. Or maybe I would –

Leader: (interrupting) You can stop right there. David's sin did cause him lots of problems. First, David and Bathsheba's son died soon after his birth. And David had loads of family problems because of his sin.

Professor: But I'm still confused. David's sins were bad, really bad, too bad for God to forgive him.

Leader: So, you think God shouldn't forgive all the kids here in kid's church?

Professor: Sure, He should forgive them – Unless they commit a big sin like adultery or murder.

Leader: What about lying? Hating? Disobeying parents? Stealing? Cheating? Fighting? Cursing? Should God forgive those things?

Professor: Little white lies – yes; big black lies – no. Cheating on a math test – yes; cheating in a football game – no. Fighting with your sister – yes; fighting with your best...

Leader: (interrupting) Hold right there and listen. Sin is sin is sin is sin. If God can forgive one sin, He can forgive every sin. The important thing is whether or not we will admit our sin and ask for God's forgiveness.

Professor: Just like King David did?

Leader: Just like King David did?

Professor: Long live the King... of Heaven! (exits)

Praise Break: Psalm 24:1-4 (Use Building a Place for God's Glory lesson 3 praise slide)

Have the children read Psalm 24:1-4 with you two to three times with feeling.

Today, let's praise God for giving us clean hands and a pure heart.

Praise and Worship: Choose a couple of fast song and a slow song to lead children into praise and worship. It works well to talk to the children about what worship is and why it's important before you enter into this time. You can have a children's praise team, but until they understand leading praise and worship, have an adult leader or yourself be the worship leader.

Object Lessons:

1. **Which Cup Would Jesus Drink From**

Supplies Needed: 2 cups - A beautiful china cup with dirt and mud and the inside and an old beat up cup that is clean on the inside. Do not allow the children to see the inside of the cups.

Children, I have two cups in front of me. If Jesus wanted a cup of water, which cup would He drink from? Let the children answer. Then show them the insides of the cups. Let them answer again.

Jesus once accused the religious leaders of His day of being like dishes that were beautiful on the outside but dirty on the inside. Once we have been saved, Jesus wants us to continue to search our hearts to see if there is any sin in us. Then He will cleanse us of our sin. If we ignore the things we do wrong, we will become like this teacup. We will look good on the outside but be full of dirt on the inside. Are you a cup that Jesus would want to take a drink from?

2. **Object Lesson #2: The Golden Basin** (use Building a Place for God's Glory lesson 3, slide B)

Supplies needed: a basin of water

In Bible days, after a priest sacrificed at the brazen altar we learned about last week, he would have to go to a golden basin and wash His hands and feet. There was nothing magical about the water, but it did remind him he needed to have a pure heart before the Lord.

We don't have to offer animal sacrifices today because Jesus sacrificed Himself for our sins. If we have accepted Jesus' sacrifice, He has forgiven our sins.

Wash your hands in the basin of water.

Even though we are Christians, we are not perfect. Sometimes we disobey the Lord. When we do, we must ask Christ to forgive our sin. Just as I am washing my hands, so Jesus washes away my sin when I confess it to Him.

Just as I don't have to get a whole bath every time I dirty my hands, so I don't have to get saved all over again when I disobey God. Instead, I need to confess that sin, let Him forgive me, and move on.

Sermon: What Well are You Drinking From

(use Building a Place for God's Glory lesson 3, slide C & D)

God wants us to have pure hearts and clean hands. A pure heart is a heart after God. Clean hands means what we do to honor God. Sin doesn't honor God, but when we sin, God wants us to confess our sin and come to Him so He can forgive us. A pure heart or a heart after God wants to confess the things they've done wrong and make it right as soon as possible.

But God wants to do more than forgive us, He wants to sanctify us. Sanctify is a big word that means the power to say yes to God and no to sin. It doesn't happen all at once, but as we grow closer to God, we gain more power to no to sin and yes to God.

When we are sanctified in an area, we no longer want to give in to the temptation to disobey our parents. Instead, we will want to say yes to God. When our parents ask us to clean our room, we will want to not only clean our room but also do the dishes. We want to help our parents.

When we are tempted to be mean to a kid at school who doesn't have any friends, instead of giving in to that temptation, we will invite the kid to eat lunch with us. We will show God's love to him.

There are a lot of temptations that try to get us to do the wrong thing, but God wants to sanctify us so we have the power to say yes to God and no to sin.

So how do we become sanctified? Jerimiah 2:13 says, "My people have committed two sins: They have forsaken me, the spring of living water, and have dug their own cisterns, broken cisterns that cannot hold water."

There are two kinds of wells we can build in our lives.

(Show slide C) *A broken cistern is a well with a crack in it. It can't hold water. In other words, we are satisfied with other things more than we a satisfied with God, it's like pouring water in a broken well. No matter how hard we try, we don't have power to say yes to God and no to sin.*

There are some things that are easy to figure out that they are broken cistern. If we are watching TV shows or playing video games with evil things in them, of course, that is a broken well, but anything can be a broken well if we are more satisfied with it than we are with God.

An example would be a friend wants us to spend the night on a Saturday night. That friend's family isn't Christian and doesn't go to church. If we want to spend the night with that friend and skip church, that would be a broken cistern, but we could ask the friend to go to church with us on Sunday and have our parents pick us up on their way. Or we could spend the night on Friday night instead. Or we could ask our friend to spend the night with us so they could go to church. Or we could go and visit but not spend the night. If we want to honor God by going to church, then we can find a way to be a friend and go to church.

(Show slide D) *God wants to satisfy us with His springs of living water. When we find our satisfaction in God, we will want to spend time in His presence. We will want to worship Him. We will want to learn about what God's Word says for our lives. We will want to be Spirit filled. We will find our greatest satisfaction in Him. The more we are satisfied with God, the more we will want to drink for His living water. He will fill us with his Spirit and with joy.*

Romans 15:13 says, "May the God of hope fill you with all joy and peace as you trust in him, so that you may overflow with hope by the power of the Holy Spirit."

So, what well are you drinking from? Are you finding the most satisfaction in things other than God, broken wells that hold no water?

If you are drinking from God's spring of living water, these are the ways you know.

You have peace and are filled with joy.

You overflow with hope.

The power of the Holy Spirit grows stronger in your life.

When you do sin, you want to make it right as soon as possible.

You gain greater power to say yes to God and no to sin.

For response time, see small group chat.

Response Time/Small Group Chat:

Use this response time in place of the small group chat.

Supplies needed: basins of water and clean towels

We can have clean hearts if we follow David's example. In a minute, I'm going to ask each of you to come up here and wash your hands in the basin. After you do, please find a place to kneel and pray.

Ask Him to search your heart and show you areas where you have not done what God wants you to. Are there areas where you've been drinking from broken cisterns?

Ask God to forgive you for the things you've done wrong.

Ask Him to create a clean heart in you.

Ask God to sanctify you by His truth. Ask Him to give you the power to say yes to God and no to sin.

At the end of this response time, have your student gather together for a time of worship where they can draw near to God and drink from His living water.

Building a Place for God's Glory Lesson 3

Clean Hands and a Pure Heart Family Devotions Handout

Memory Verse: Psalm 24:3b-4a *Who may stand in his holy place? The one who has clean hands and a pure heart...*

Summary: Sanctification is a big word that basically means saying yes to God and no to sin. We do that by having clean hands and a pure heart. That means when we do mess up, we ask God to forgive us, then we don't do it again.

This sheet is provided to help families with devotions to go with the lessons your children learned in children's church this week. Included is a daily Bible reading to use for discussions.

Monday: Read 2 Samuel 12:1-13. David messed up big, but when God sent Nathan to rebuke him, he confessed and repented of his sin. That's why David was called a man after God's own heart.

Tuesday: Read Exodus 40:30-32. God told Moses to place a golden laver before the Holy Place of the temple. Before the priests entered God's presence, they washed their hands. We should also examine ourselves often to allow God to wash our hands and heart of anything that doesn't please Him.

Wednesday: Read 2 Timothy 2:20-21. God wants us to have clean hands and a pure heart because He has a purpose for us.

Thursday: Read Colossians 3:1-2. We become sanctified by setting our hearts and minds on Christ.

Friday: Read 1 Thessalonians 5:23. God wants to sanctify us in Him.

Saturday: Read Psalm 16:11. God wants us to find our greatest satisfaction in Him. When we do, He fills us with His joy.

Family Activity: Spending Time Together

Supplies needed: None

Do something with your children that they love to do. That will be different for every family, but it should be something you can all do together.

At the end of the activity, tell them you really loved spending time with them. Ask them if they had fun. Tell them that God wants them to spend time in His presence. When they find their satisfaction in Him, He fills them with joy. Spending time with God is fun, and they can have joy having fun doing things, knowing God is with them.

Lesson 4: The Word of God Brings Revival

Focus Point: The table of Showbread represents the Word of God, both the Bible and who the Bible points to – Jesus Christ.

Goal: Children will have a desire to know the Word of God.

Focus Verse: *Then Jesus declared, "I am the Bread of Life. He who comes to me will never go hungry, and he who believes in Me will never be thirsty"* John 6:35

Supplies Needed:

- Building a Place for God Videos (free with registration)
- Building a Place for God Jpeg Slides (free with registration)
- copies of Building a Place for God Family Devotional Sheet
- Professor Confuzed costume: lab coat or a shirt with a pocket protector
- 2 loaves of bread
- Alphabet cereal (You may have to use more than one box to make sure all the letters are there.) You can substitute alphabet magnets, blocks, or construction paper letters.
- a glass of water
- red, green, yellow and blue food coloring
- chlorine bleach
- clean towels
- rechargeable battery
- table
- mirror
- candy bar
- snacks for students

Opening: *Building a Place for God's Glory Countdown* or *Building a Place for God's Glory* Intro Slide (Available free with registration of this curriculum.)

Welcome: *Oh, I am so hungry, this morning. I didn't have breakfast, and my stomach is growling. Children, have you ever felt hungry before? Even though I hungry, I'm not really that hungry. For instance, I hate (name a food). If somebody were to offer me that food, I wouldn't eat it. But if I had gone without food for months and was starving to death and had no way to get any food like some children are in this world right now, I would eat anything, even _____. God wants us to be hungry like that, but not for food. He wants us to be hungry for Him and His Word.*

Prayer: Ask a child to pray over the service.

Rules: (use rules slide)

Go over the *5 Ups Rules*: 1. Sit up straight. 2. Listen up. 3. Hush up. 4. Don't get up and run around or go to the bathroom. 5. Worship Up! (stand and participate during praise and worship)

Theme or Activity Songs: Choose one or two fast moving activity songs that goes with the curriculum.

Game Time: Eating Contest (use game time slide)

Supplies needed: A loaf of bread

Choose three to six children to participate. Give each child 3 slices of bread. The first child to eat and swallow all three slices wins. To keep this game from being a choking hazard, children must eat one slice at a time and swallow it all, then drink a sip of water, before they can eat another slice.

Offering: Manna From Heaven

Sometimes people worry about giving too large of an offering to God because their afraid they might not have enough for themselves. They are thinking about offering in the wrong way. We give, not because God needs our money, but to show we understand everything is God's, and God provided everything we have.

In Exodus, Moses and the Israelites were in the desert and didn't have enough to eat. Every day, God provided for them by sending manna from Heaven. If God took care of the Israelites with bread from Heaven, He'll provide us with everything we need.

Memory Verse: *Then Jesus declared, "I am the Bread of Life. He who comes to me will never go hungry, and he who believes in Me will never be thirsty" John 6:35*

Memory Verse Talk: (use Building a Place for God's Glory lesson 4, slide A)

I've been thinking a lot about today's verse. Then Jesus declared, "I am the Bread of Life. He who comes to me will never go hungry, and he who believes in Me will never be thirsty." John 6:35. Jesus said He's the bread of life, but that doesn't we should eat Him like bread. That would be ridiculous. And He certainly doesn't mean we should go without food or water. I would get mighty thirsty and hungry if I had to do that.

Jesus isn't talking about physical bread. He's talking about spiritual bread. He is the Word of God, and we find His words in the Bible. That's why, in Matthew 4:4, Jesus said, "Man shall not live on bread alone, but on every word that comes from the mouth of God." So. if we read and study the Bible, we are feeding our spirits. When we feed our spirits with Jesus, the Word of God, we won't starve spiritually. I can't wait to read more of God's Word and feed my spirit.

Memory Verse Activity: Food Spelling Bee

Supplies needed: Alphabet cereal (You may have to use more than one box to make sure all the letters are there.) You can substitute alphabet magnets, blocks, or construction paper letters.

Have two teams. Each team races to find the letters of the memory verse and put them in the right order on a table. The first team to complete the verse wins.

Skit: Professor Confuzed Gets Hungry

Professor Confuzed: Hello everyone.

Leader: Well, hello, Professor Confuzed. How are you doing today?

Professor: I was doing pretty good, but now I am terrible.

Leader: Why are you terrible, Professor?

Professor: I haven't eaten for a while and I'm so hungry.

Leader: How long has it been since you've eaten?

Professor: Three days and I'm starved.

Leader: Professor, why haven't you eaten in three days. I know that you have plenty of food in your refrigerator.

Professor: You should know. It's your fault.

Leader: Professor, I don't understand. Why is it my fault that you haven't eaten in three days?

Professor: Do you remember the other day when you came over to my house?

Leader: Yes, Professor, I remember.

Professor: Do you remember how you told me what you were going to preach on in children's church?

Leader: I remember.

Professor: Do you remember reading John 6:35 to me?

Leader: I remember that too.

Professor: Ah, ha, so you admit it. It's all your fault.

Leader: Professor, I don't understand. How did coming over to your house and telling you what I was preaching in children's church and reading John 6:35 cause you not to eat for three days.

Professor: John 6:35 says that Jesus is the Bread of Life and if we come to Him, we will never go hungry.

Leader: Yes, go on.

Professor: When's the last time you've ever seen Jesus.

Leader: I've never actually seen Jesus in person, but I've felt Him in my spirit.

Professor: Ah, ha.

Leader: Again with the ah, ha. Professor, what are you talking about? I'm confused.

Professor: You're confused? I've been looking for Jesus for three days so I wouldn't be hungry. Well I couldn't find Him, and I am very hungry. I'm about ready to stop looking for Jesus and get something to eat. I don't know why I ever listened to you.

Leader: Professor, you're confused.

Professor: I'm confused. Who told me to stop eating?

Leader: Professor, I didn't tell you to stop eating. That verse doesn't mean we should stop eating and look for Jesus so that He can feed us physically. It means that we need to hunger and thirst for God and His Word and come to Jesus by reading the Word of God. Then He will fill us spiritually. It has nothing to do with eating food.

Professor: Why didn't you say so in the first place? I think you're a little bit confused.

Leader: I'm afraid not one who's confused.

Professor: I'm going to go now. I am going to go get something to eat. Then I'm going to read my Bible.

Leader: That's a good idea. That will fill you up physically and spiritually. Good-bye, Professor. Children just as it's important to physically eat, it is important to eat spiritually by reading God's Word.

Object Lessons:

1. Renew Your Mind (Romans 12:2)

Supplies Needed: bread, table, a glass of water, red, green, yellow and blue food coloring, chlorine bleach

When talking about the table of shewbread, it might be a good opportunity to take communion with the students.

Show table with bread.

After a person went to the brazen altar and to the golden laver, he could enter the holy place. There he would find a table with bread on it. The bread shows us that if we want the presence of God in our lives, we have to fill our hearts and minds with His Word. To keep our hearts pure, we have to be careful what we allow in our minds.

We all live in a sinful world where bad thoughts are constantly trying to be put in our minds. Television, music, books, video games, and even friends can sometimes give messages to us that are ungodly. If we listen to these messages and allow them to influence us, we will start to have bad thoughts.

For instance, if somebody does something wrong to me, I might become angry and bitter. Pour a drop of red food coloring in the glass and stir it.

Then I might become jealous of anything good that happens to that person. Pour a drop of green food coloring into the glass and stir it up.

I might even start to lie and gossip about that person. Put a drop of yellow food coloring in the glass and stir it up.

Finally, I would probably become blue or sad and depressed because of all the wrong thinking you have been doing. Put a drop of blue food coloring in the glass and stir it up. Hold the glass up.

At this point, your mind is a mess. What can you do?

Romans 12:2 tells us that we shouldn't have the same kind of thinking that the world has but that we should change our thinking by renewing our minds. We can do that by filling our minds with the Word of God and meditating or thinking about God's Word. When we do that, our minds will be cleansed of all the filth of the world and we can begin to think like Jesus.

Pour a large amount of bleach into the glass and stir it up. *Our minds and thoughts will be renewed by God's Word.*

2. Recharging Your Battery

Supplies Needed: rechargeable battery

Show a rechargeable battery. Talk about how the battery will only last so long then it needs to be recharged. Our spirits are the same way. When we study and think about God's Word every day, we are recharging our spiritual batteries.

3. The Mirror of God's Word

Supplies needed: mirror

James 1:23-25 ICB says "A person who hears God's teaching and does nothing is like a man looking in a mirror. He sees his face, then goes away and quickly forgets what he looked like. But the truly happy person is the one who carefully studies God's perfect law that makes people free. He continues to study it. He listens to God's teaching and does not forget what he heard. Then he obeys what God's teaching says. When he does this, it makes him happy.

Show mirror. *According to these verses, a person who hears or reads the Bible but ignores what it says is like someone who looks in this mirror. Maybe that person has a smudge on his nose, but he doesn't wipe it off. Instead, he walks away and forgets what he saw. Maybe someone looks in the mirror and sees her hair is messy. She doesn't comb or brush it or put product in it. Instead she walks away and forgets her hair is messy.*

The Bible is like a mirror. We can read it or listen to it, but it won't do any good unless we study it, think about it often, and obey what it says. When we do this, not only does it please God, it makes us happy.

God's Word satisfies us in a way nothing else can.

Praise Break: Towdah (Use Building a Place for God's Glory lesson 4 praise slide.)

For the next 7 weeks, during the praise break, children will be learning different words for praise in the Bible and what they mean. Have the children repeat the word Towdah (pronounced Toda).

Towdah means to extend the hands in acceptance or agreement with God's words and promises before you see them answered. It's used in Psalm 42:4 "…I went with them to the house of God, with the voice of joy and praise…"

Have the children give testimonies about things they are thankful for.

Praise and Worship: Choose a couple of fast song and a slow song to lead children into praise and worship. It works well to talk to the children about what worship is and why it's important before you enter into this time. You can have a children's praise team, but until they understand leading praise and worship, have an adult leader or yourself be the worship leader.

Bible Story: God's Word Brings Revival (Nehemiah 8:1-6)

Tell this story using your own words. First tell the story of how God's Word brought revival in the days of Ezra. Then tell about how God's Word brings revival even today. If you have ever been in a church in revival, give a testimony about your experience.

In the days of Ezra, nobody knew the Word of God. Ezra had them gather in the square by the water gate. Ezra read the Scripture out loud from early morning until noon. All the people listened very closly. Then something amazing happened. In Nehemiah 8:6 it says, Ezra praised the Lord, the great God. And all the people held up their hands and said, "Amen! Amen!" Then they bowed down and worshiped the Lord with their faces to the ground. God brought revival to the Israelites through the reading of God's Word.

Reformation: One of the greatest moves of God happened when Martin Luther read the Bible and discovered the Biblical truth that salvation comes through faith in God.

First Great Awakening: During the first Great Awakening (American revival), Jonathan Edwards, minister, took apart the pages of his Bible and put it back together with blank pages in between each page so he could write notes about what he was learning during his studies. He studied Scripture every day, some days as much as twelve hours a day. George Whitefield, evangelist, said, "I began to read the Holy Scriptures upon my knees… This proved meat indeed and drink indeed to my soul. I daily received fresh light and power from above."

Second Great Awakening: Charles Finney, evangelist, said, "The spirit of the whole Bible breathes from every page…"

Third Great Awakening: The third Great Awakening started in Chicago when DL Moody decided to have a Bible study for children.

Azusa Street Pentecostal Revival: William J. Seymour started this revival after learning about what Scripture said about being baptized in the Holy Spirit.

There have been many more revivals throughout history, but true revivals will always be based on the Word of God.

Sermon: Are You Hungry

(Use Building a Place for God's Glory lesson 4, slides B-G)

Supplies needed: candy bar

Preach this sermon in your own words using these notes.

Eat a candy bar in front of the children. Say things like, "mmm, this is so good." When the children respond, ask them if they are hungry.

I'm glad you're hungry. We shouldn't only be hungry for food though. We should also be hungry for God. Sometimes we aren't hungry because of things that kill our hunger.

Hunger Killers:

Sickness – sin, not saved

Snacking – filled up with other things so there's no room for God.

Matthew 5:6 says, *Blessed are those who hunger and thirst for righteousness, because they will be filled. God wants to prepare us a spiritual meal.*

God Prepares a Meal:

Appetizer: (Use Slide B) Psalm 34:8 *Taste and see that the Lord is good; blessed is the one who takes refuge in him.* (Salvation, Walking with God)

Water: (Use Slide C) Psalm 42:1-2 *As the deer pants for the water brooks, So my soul pants for You, O God. My soul thirsts for God, for the living God; When shall I come and appear before God?*

John 4:14 *But whoever drinks of the water that I will give him shall never thirst; but the water that I will give him will become in him a well of water springing up to eternal life.".* (Jesus is the water of life, Holy Spirit)

John 7:37-39 *Now on the last day, the great day of the feast, Jesus stood and cried out, saying, "If anyone is thirsty, let him come to Me and drink. "He who believes in Me, as the Scripture said, 'From his innermost being will flow rivers of living water.'" But this He spoke of the Spirit, whom those who believed in Him were to receive; for the Spirit was not yet given, because Jesus was not yet glorified.* (believe on Jesus, Holy Spirit, Joy)

Isaiah 44:3 *For I will pour out water on the thirsty land And streams on the dry ground; I will pour out My Spirit on your offspring And My blessing on your descendants.* (Holy Spirit, blessings)

Meal:

Bread: (Use slide D) John 6:35 *Jesus said to them, "I am the bread of life; he who comes to Me will not hunger, and he who believes in Me will never thirst.* (Spending time with Jesus)

Milk: (Use Slide E) 1 Peter 2:2 *Like newborn babies, long for the pure milk of the word, so that by it you may grow in respect to salvation.* (learning God's Word)

Solid Food or Meat: (Use Slide F) Hebrew 5:14 *Solid food is for the mature, who because of practice have their senses trained to discern good and evil.*

Desert: (Use Slide G) Psalm 37:4 *Delight yourself in the LORD; And He will give you the desires of your heart.*

Have children come forward. Lay hands on each of them. Pray for them to be hungry for God's Word, respond to God's Word, study God's Word and obey God's Word so that God's presence will be in their lives.

Small Group Chat:

Supplies Needed: Snack

If you normally have snacks, wait until the small group chat to have them. Bread sticks or pretzels would work well. As the children are eating, ask them what their favorite foods are. Ask them if they've ever been really hungry. Talk about the importance of being hungry for God.

Building a Place for God's Glory Lesson 4

The Word of God Brings Revival Family Devotions Handout

Memory Verse: John 6:35 *Then Jesus declared, "I am the Bread of Life. He who comes to me will never go hungry, and he who believes in Me will never be thirsty"*

Summary: Revival and refreshing comes from being hungry for God's Word.

This sheet is provided to help families with devotions to go with the lessons your children learned in children's church this week. Included is a daily Bible reading to use for discussions.

Monday: Read Romans 12:2. Discuss ways to renew your mind using God's Word.

Tuesday: Read James 1:23-25. How is reading the Bible and not obeying it like looking in a mirror and forgetting what you see?

Wednesday: Read Nehemiah 8:1-6. How is the way we treat God's Word different than in Ezra's time?

Thursday: Read 1 Peter 2:2. How can we long for God's Word like a baby longs for milk?

Friday: Read Hebrews 5:14. The food this verse is talking about is God's Word. How do we become mature in God's Word?

Saturday: Read Deuteronomy 8:3. What does this verse say about God's Word?

Family Activity: Family Meal

Go to your kids' favorite restaurant or make a family meal and eat it at the dinner table. Afterwards have a conversation about the food and talk about how the Bible is our spiritual food.

Lesson 5: How To Be a Fruity Christian

Focus Point: The fruit in the golden candlestick that holds the oil represents the fruit of the Spirit that should be in every Christian.

Goal: Children will learn that the more they are attached to Christ the more they will reflect God in their lives.

Focus Verse: *I am the vine; you are the branches. If you remain in me and I in you, you will bear much fruit; apart from me you can do nothing.* John 15:5

Supplies needed:

- Building a Place for God Videos (free with registration)
- Building a Place for God Jpeg Slides (free with registration)
- copies of Building a Place for God Family Devotional Sheet
- Professor Confuzed costume: lab coat or a shirt with a pocket protector
- construction paper with shapes of fruit cut out
- template for cutouts (from sheet at the end of this lesson)
- snacks for students
- scotch tap
- Fruity Christian Video (free with registration)
- flower or a branch with blossoms on it
- fruit snack

Opening: *Building a Place for God's Glory Countdown* or *Building a Place for God's Glory* Intro Slide (Available free with registration of this curriculum.)

Welcome: *How many of you are fruity Christians? I don't mean how many of you are crazy. When I say fruity Christian, I mean a Christian who has the fruit of the Spirit showing in his or her life. Today, we're going to learn how to be fruity Christians.*

Prayer: Ask a child to pray over the service.

Rules: (use rules slide)

Go over the *5 Ups Rules*: 1. Sit up straight. 2. Listen up. 3. Hush up. 4. Don't get up and run around or go to the bathroom. 5. Worship Up! (stand and participate during praise and worship)

Theme or Activity Songs: Choose one or two fast moving activity songs that goes with the curriculum.

Game Time: Fruit Basket (use game time slide)

Supplies Needed: One chair for each child in a circle.

Stand in the middle of the circle. Assign each child a fruit: banana, pear, apple, grapes. The more students playing the game, the greater number of fruits. Explain the rules. When the person in the center calls the name of a fruit, everyone who is assigned that fruit jumps up and changes chairs. The student without a chair stands in the middle and calls the next fruit.

The first time you play the game, take your place in one of the chairs. After a couple of rounds, stand up and go to the center. Explain that when someone says "fruit basket", everyone changes seats, but they are not allowed to sit in the seat on either side of them. Say "fruit basket", find a seat, and continue the game.

Memory Verse: *I am the vine; you are the branches. If you remain in me and I in you, you will bear much fruit; apart from me you can do nothing.* John 15:5

Memory Verse Talk: (use Building a Place for God's Glory lesson 5, slide A)

A grape vine has many branches, but if one of them is cut off, it won't grow any grapes. Eventually it will die. That's the way it is with us spiritually. As long as we remain attached to Jesus, we will produce the fruit of the Spirit. The fruit of the Spirit is love, joy, peace, forbearance, kindness, goodness, faithfulness, gentleness, and self-control. It's not nine different fruits but one fruit that acts this way. With this fruit, we act more like Jesus, but when we go our own way or try to do things on our own, we will whiter spiritually.

Memory Verse Activity: Fruity Relay

Supplies needed: Cut out shapes of fruit with each word of the memory verse on it (See the page at the end of this lesson for a template to cut out the fruit.), scotch tape

Divide the children into two teams. Give each child one piece of paper or poster board. When you say go, instruct the children to stand so that the words of the verse are in order with the verse reference last. The first team to put the verse in order wins.

Puppets or Skit: Fruity Christian or Just Fruity

Professor Confuzed: Hello, everyone. I'm so happy to be here today.

Leader: Why are you so happy to be here today, Professor Confuzed?

Professor: I'm so happy to be here because I heard that you are talking about fruity Christians.

Leader: Why does that make you happy, Professor?

Professor: This is a subject on which I have a lot of experience.

Leader: Really, Professor. I didn't know that you had so much experience with the fruit of the Spirit.

Lesson 5: How To Be a Fruity Christian

Professor: I don't.

Leader: But you said you have a lot of experience.

Professor: That's right. People have told me that I'm as fruity as a fruitcake for years. Therefore, I know a lot about being fruity.

Leader: Professor, you're a bit confused. We're not talking about being fruity the way people tell you that you are fruity.

Professor: I don't understand. You said we should be fruit.

Leader: Yes, I know, but I was talking about the fruit of the Spirit.

Professor: Is there a spirit of fruit? I didn't know that.

Leader: No, Professor, not the spirit of fruit. I'm talking about the fruit that the Holy Spirit produces in Christians.

Professor: Do you mean that if I become a Christian, God is going to grow fruit on me?

Leader: Yes, in a way, He is.

Professor: That is so great. Why didn't you tell me this? I want Him to grow apples on me. I love big, red, juicy apples.

Leader: That not the kind of fruit I meant.

Professor: How about pears or peaches or pineapples? I like fruits that begin with the letter P.

Leader: No Professor. The kind of fruit that the Holy Spirit grows is spiritual fruit, not physical fruit.

Professor: What's spiritual fruit? I never heard of that kind of fruit.

Leader: Spiritual fruit is love, joy, peace, patience, kindness, goodness, faithfulness, gentleness and self-control.

Professor: Nobody is that good.

Leader: On our own, that is true, but if we stay connected to God, He will produce spiritual fruit in us. He is the vine and we are the branches. We have to stay connected to Him to grow spiritual fruit.

Professor: I think I'm beginning to understand, but I have to go now. I heard we were talking about fruit, so I planted some apple trees in the back yard. I have been watering them for three days, and I think they might be wet enough by now.

Leader: Oh Professor, you're so confused. Kids, some people that if they try hard enough, they can be good enough to please God. God doesn't want us to try harder. He just wants us to grow closer to Him. Then we will grow the fruit of the Spirit in our lives.

Offering: Faithful Giving

One of the fruit of the spirit is faithfulness. It is important to be faithful in our giving. That's why we should pay tithe, ten percent, of everything we earn or are given every time we receive any money. Explain how much ten percent is by giving examples.

Video: Fruity Christians

(Available free with registration of this curriculum.)

Bible Story: Peter Becomes Fruity (Luke 22:54-62; Acts 2)

Before Peter was baptized in the Holy Spirit, He always tried hard to say the right things, but he was always saying the wrong things. He tried hard to have faith. He even got out of the boat and walked on water, but then his faith failed, and he sank.

Peter wanted to be Jesus' right hand man. Before Jesus was arrested, Peter declared that even if everyone else denied Jesus, he would die with Him. He meant what he said. He wanted to follow Jesus to the end. When the soldiers came to arrest Jesus, Peter picked up a sword and cut off a guard's ear. Jesus had to stop Peter from defending Him to the death. It seemed like Peter was really going to follow Jesus no matter what.

Peter couldn't keep it up. In the courtyard, while Jesus was facing His accusers, Peter was challenged three times. People said they were sure he was with Jesus and was one of His followers. Each time, Peter was afraid and denied that he even knew Jesus. The last time, he even swore and yelled at the people that he didn't know Jesus. Then a rooster crowed, and Peter remember that Jesus said he would deny Him. Peter was very upset. No matter how hard he tried, Peter could not always do the right thing.

When Peter was baptized in the Holy Spirit, he was connected to God and had the fruit of the Spirit growing in Him. He became a fruity Christian. Not only was Peter not afraid of people, he preached a sermon to a great crowd in which three thousand people were saved. Another time, he was facing Roman authorities who told him that they would kill him if he kept preaching about Jesus. Peter told them that he was going to obey God rather than man.

Without relying on God, Peter couldn't even stay true to God in front of a small group of people, but when he did rely on God, God used him in mighty ways to speak to great crowds, and many people were saved.

Praise Break: Halel

(Use Building a Place for God's Glory lesson 5 praise slide)

This week, during the praise break, children will be learning the next word for praise in the Bible and what it means. Have the children repeat the word Halel (pronounced Ha lil).

Halel means to go wild over like at a baseball game when your team hits a home run and everybody goes jumps and claps and yells. We can praise God by celebrating and going crazy or fruity over Him. It's used in Psalm 150:2. "Praise him for his mighty acts."

Have the children give testimonies about things they are thankful for.

Praise and Worship: Choose a couple of fast song and a slow song to lead children into praise and worship. It works well to talk to the children about what worship is and why it's important before you enter into this time. You can have a children's praise team, but until they understand leading praise and worship, have an adult leader or yourself be the worship leader.

Object Lessons:

1. Connected To the Vine (John 15:1-8)

Supplies Needed: flower or a branch with blossoms on it

Boys and girls, on the way to church I picked this beautiful flower (or branch with blossoms). I think that it is so pretty. In fact, I'm going to take it home with me and plant it in some dirt and water it so that it will grow. Don't you think that's a good idea?

Let your students tell you that the flower will die.

I don't understand. If I water this flower and take care of it, why would it die?

Let the children explain that when a flower is not connected to the plant it will die.

Do you mean to tell me that when this flower stopped being connected to the plant, it started to die? You know, that's a lot like Christians. As long as we are connected to God in a relationship with Him, we show the fruit of the Spirit in our lives, but when we stop being connected to God and we start to allow our relationship with Him to suffer, we stop being fruity Christians, and we begin to die spiritually.

Read John 15:1-8.

Let's stay connected to God so that we can be fruity Christians.

2. The Golden Candlestick Cups

(Use Building a Place for God's Glory lesson 5, slide B)

In the Holy Place in the Tabernacle, the priest would be able to see what he was doing because of a golden candlestick called a menorah. The menorah had nine cup holders where the oil was poured. Each cup holder was in the shape of an almond. An almond in those days was considered a fruit. Just as the candlestick represents the Holy Spirit, the almonds represent the fruit of the Holy Spirit. In order to be in the presence of God, we need to be connected to Him so that we can be fruity Christians.

Sermon: How to Be a Fruity Christian

Many people try hard to be good enough, but the Bible says that without God, you can do nothing. The closer you are to God, the more His light will shine through you. Then you can have the fruit of the Spirit in you. Just as a branch that is connected to the tree produces fruit, if you are connected to God, you will produce the fruit of the Spirit.

Let's look at the fruit of the Spirit that will flow through you when you grow close to God.

Love: This means that you will love everyone, even those who treat you mean.

Joy: Joy is an inner happiness that is there even when you have lots of problems.

Peace: Peace is a calmness that happens on the inside when we trust in God and keep our minds on Him.

Longsuffering: Longsuffering is patience to endure trouble or pain even for a long time without getting frustrated or angry.

Kindness: Kindness is treating other people like you would like to be treated.

Goodness: Goodness is doing what is right even when it is hard.

Faithfulness: A faithful person is a person who is loyal. He is a person that God and other people can trust.

Gentleness: Gentleness is treating others with gentleness, respect and kindness.

Self-Control: Self-control is when a person can control the way he or she acts or thinks.

Nobody can act that way all the time without the power of the Holy Spirit in them. That's why we need to be connected to Jesus.

Have any children who would like to be connected to God so that they can be fruity Christians come forward to be prayed for. Lay hands on each child's head and pray for that student to remain connected to Jesus.

Small Group Chat:

Supplies needed: fruit snack

Serve the children for a fruit for a snack. Ask them their favorite kind of fruit. Talk about how fruit is a very healthy snack, but just as fruit makes us physically healthy, the fruit of the Spirit shows other people how we are spiritually healthy. Talk to the children about how they can be connected to Jesus so that the fruit of the Spirit shows in them.

Memory Verse Activity from Lesson 5

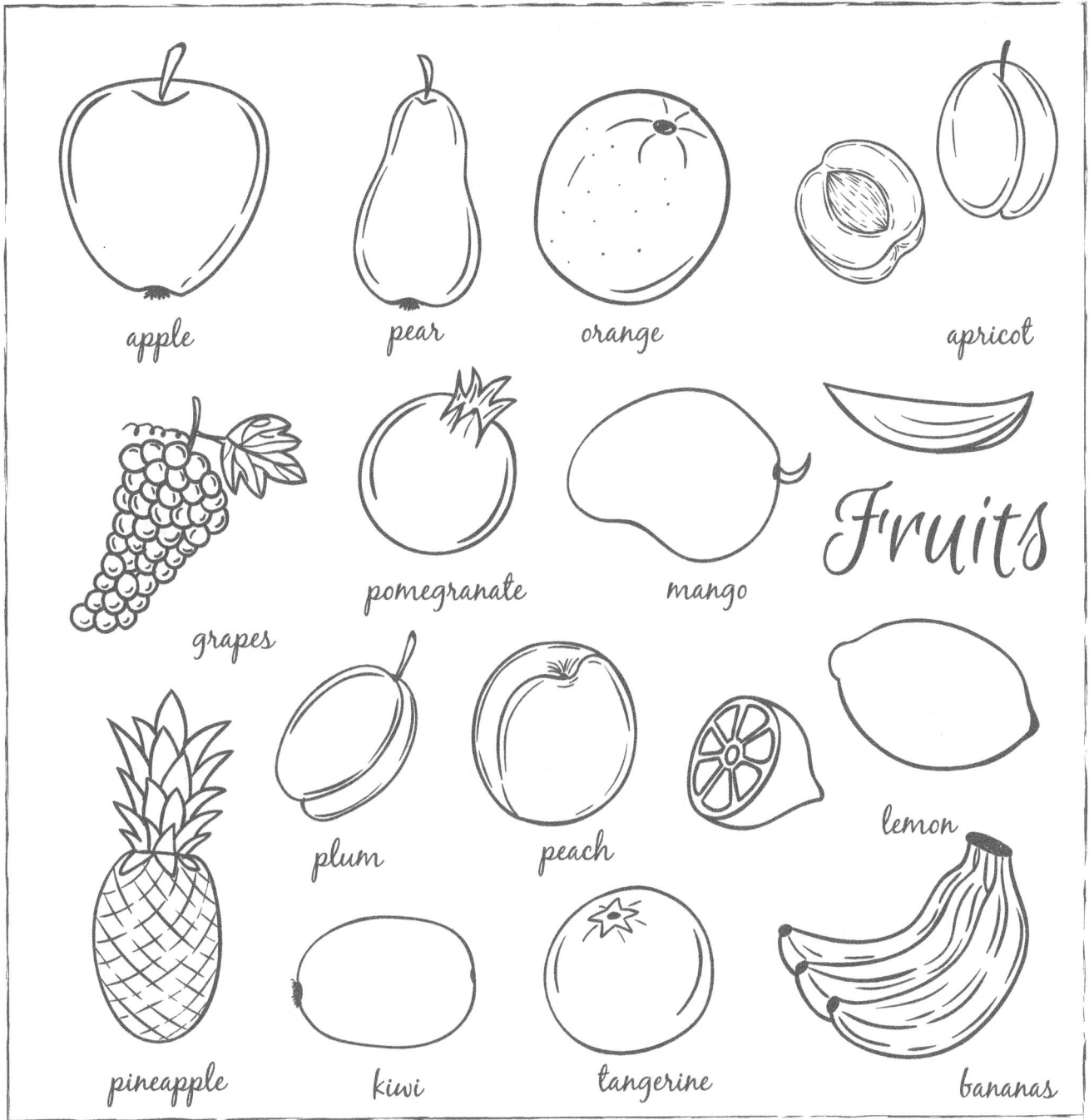

Building a Place for God's Glory Lesson 5

Fruity Christians Family Devotions Handout

Memory Verse: John 15:5 *I am the vine; you are the branches. If you remain in me and I in you, you will bear much fruit; apart from me you can do nothing.*

Summary: The fruit of the Spirit is not different characteristics we have to work at to incorporate in our lives. The fruit of the Spirit is one fruit. It is produced by being attached to God through the Holy Spirit.

This sheet is provided to help families with devotions to go with the lessons your children learned in children's church this week. Included is a daily Bible reading to use for discussions.

Monday: Read John 15:1-8. Talk about staying connected to Jesus.

Tuesday: Read Galatians 2:22-23. Talk about the fruit of the Holy Spirit. We can't show this fruit unless we are connected to Jesus.

Wednesday: Read Jeremiah 31:3; Romans 15:13. These verses talk about love, joy, and peace.

Thursday: Read Romans 2:4; Colossians 3:12-13. How God show longsuffering and kindness toward us? How can we show this fruit toward others?

Friday: Read Galatians 6:10; Hebrews 10:33. How can we show goodness to others? How has God been faithful to us?

Saturday: Read Proverbs 15:11; James 1:26. How can we show gentleness toward others with our words? What is the most important thing to use self-control with?

Family Activity: Random Acts of Kindness

Supplies needed: See next page for Random Acts of Kindness Cards

Create random acts of Kindness Cards using template from next page. Encourage your children to do random acts of kindness throughout the week for others and give them the card when they do. Parents, this works better if you participate too. At the end of the week, discuss these random acts of kindness.

Random Act of Kindness	Random Act of Kindness	Random Act of Kindness
John 3:16 *For God so loved the world that He gave His only begotten Son, that whoever believes in Him should not perish but have everlasting life.*	John 3:16 *For God so loved the world that He gave His only begotten Son, that whoever believes in Him should not perish but have everlasting life.*	John 3:16 *For God so loved the world that He gave His only begotten Son, that whoever believes in Him should not perish but have everlasting life.*
Random Act of Kindness	Random Act of Kindness	Random Act of Kindness
John 3:16 *For God so loved the world that He gave His only begotten Son, that whoever believes in Him should not perish but have everlasting life.*	John 3:16 *For God so loved the world that He gave His only begotten Son, that whoever believes in Him should not perish but have everlasting life.*	John 3:16 *For God so loved the world that He gave His only begotten Son, that whoever believes in Him should not perish but have everlasting life.*
Random Act of Kindness	Random Act of Kindness	Random Act of Kindness
John 3:16 *For God so loved the world that He gave His only begotten Son, that whoever believes in Him should not perish but have everlasting life.*	John 3:16 *For God so loved the world that He gave His only begotten Son, that whoever believes in Him should not perish but have everlasting life.*	John 3:16 *For God so loved the world that He gave His only begotten Son, that whoever believes in Him should not perish but have everlasting life.*
Random Act of Kindness	Random Act of Kindness	Random Act of Kindness
John 3:16 *For God so loved the world that He gave His only begotten Son, that whoever believes in Him should not perish but have everlasting life.*	John 3:16 *For God so loved the world that He gave His only begotten Son, that whoever believes in Him should not perish but have everlasting life.*	John 3:16 *For God so loved the world that He gave His only begotten Son, that whoever believes in Him should not perish but have everlasting life.*

Lesson 6: The Oil of Anointing

Focus Point: The oil in the cups of the candlestick represent the anointing or enabling of the Holy Spirit.

Goal: Children will understand that God will enable them to do anything He has called them to do.

Focus Verse: *I can do all things through Christ who strengthens me.* Philippians 4:13 NKJV

Supplies Needed:

- Building a Place for God Videos (free with registration)
- Building a Place for God Jpeg Slides (free with registration)
- copies of Building a Place for God Family Devotional Sheet
- Professor Confuzed costume: lab coat or a shirt with a pocket protector
- one glass of water for each student participating
- one cup measuring cup for each student
- one straw for each student
- beach ball or playground ball
- jar
- rocks
- sand
- water
- slingshot (optional)
- five pieces of paper wadded up to be stones
- theme music to Rocky (optional)
- candlestick
- candle
- lighter
- three poster boards with the following written on them or three pieces of flash paper. #1- I'm not old enough to be used of God. #2 - I'm not good enough to be used by God. #3 - I don't have enough faith
- bottle of oil
- plastic sheet or plastic pool

Opening: *Building a Place for God's Glory Countdown* or *Building a Place for God's Glory* Intro Slide (Available free with registration of this curriculum.)

Welcome: *Today, we are going to talk about something called the anointing. Does anyone know what the anointing is?* Have the children answer. *The anointing is empowerment from God. In other words, the anointing is God's strength in us to do what He wants us to do.*

Prayer: Ask a child to pray over the service.

Rules: (use rules slide)

Lesson 6: The Oil of Anointing

Go over the *5 Ups Rules*: 1. Sit up straight. 2. Listen up. 3. Hush up. 4. Don't get up and run around or go to the bathroom. 5. Worship Up! (stand and participate during praise and worship)

Theme or Activity Songs: Choose one or two fast moving activity songs that goes with the curriculum.

Game Time: Impossible Task (use game time slide)

Supplies needed: one glass of water for each student participating, one cup measuring cup for each student, one straw for each student

Depending on the number of students you have, you may want to only have a few students participate while the others cheer them on. Don't allow students to see the straws yet.

How many of you believe you could fill this measuring cup using the water from this glass? Allow them to answer. *How many of you think you could do it without every touching the glass or the measuring cup?* Allow them to answer. *Most of you think it is impossible, but I'm going to show you how.* Show the straws and demonstrate.

When you put your finger over the end of a straw, you create a vacuum within the straw, strong enough to keep the liquid from slipping out the other end. Place the straw in the water, cover the end with your finger, and move the soda to the measuring cup until you reach your goal.

Have a race to fill the measuring cup. Whoever fills it first wins.

Memory Verse: *I can do all things through Christ who strengthens me.* Philippians 4:13 NKJV

Memory Verse Talk: (use Building a Place for God's Glory lesson 6, slide A)

Most people don't understand this verse. They think God will give them the power they need to do anything. Sometimes a student won't study for a test and prays God drops in knowledge to pass the test. Sometimes an athlete will think he can run a marathon without working hard to practice because God will give him all the strength he needs. God gives us all the strength we need to do what He wants us to do and to help us get through difficult times. He is not a genie in a bottle that gives us whatever we want nor can we have His strength without being filled with His Spirit.

Memory Verse Activity: Memory Verse Beach Ball

Supplies needed: 1 beach ball or playground ball.

Have two children who can recite the memory verse, come up front. Explain to the children that they are to bounce the ball to each other. As they bounce the ball, they are to say the next word of the memory verse until every word of the verse is said. Repeat with two more children as often as you have time for.

Puppets or Skit: Professor Confuzed and the Oil

Professor Confuzed: Hello boys and girls.

Leader: Hello, Professor Confuzed. How have you been lately?

Professor: Not very well and it's your fault.

Leader: I'm sorry, Professor, if I've done something to offend you? But what did I do?

Professor: You have been talking about the anointing oil and how it will give you power and strength to do things.

Leader: That's true. But what's wrong?

Professor: Yesterday I went to take my driver's test.

Leader: Really, did you pass?

Professor: No, I didn't, thanks to you.

Leader: Professor, I'm confused. How did I cause you to fail your driver's test?

Professor: Well you know that this is the seventh time I took the test.

Leader: No, Professor, I didn't. But go on.

Professor: You were talking about the anointing oil and how the anointing gives you strength to do even the impossible.

Leader: Yes, that's true.

Professor: I really wanted my driver's license, so I poured a whole bottle of oil on me. Not only did it not help me pass the test, the steering wheel was so slippery that my hands slid off of it and I ran into a police cruiser while I was taking the test. Now I have to go to court and pay a fine, and they won't let me take another driver's test for six months. It's all your fault.

Leader: Professor, you are confused. The oil is just a symbol for the anointing. It isn't really the anointing.

Professor: Now he (she) tells me.

Leader: Professor, the anointing is the strength that God gives us to do what He wants us to do. If God gives us something to do, like loving someone who treats us mean, He will give us the strength to do it, if we ask Him to. That's why I can do all things through Christ who gives me strength. It has nothing to do with pouring oil on ourselves.

Professor: Maybe I am confused. Of course, I am Professor Confuzed. So, if God wants me to have a driver's license, I just have to pray, and He will help me pass my test.

Leader: You do have to do your part like practicing your driving, but yes, He will help you.

Professor: I never tried praying or practicing my driving. Do you really think that will help?

Leader: I know it will, Professor. And now you have six months to pray and practice.

Professor: I think I'll try that. Well I have to go now. I have to find a girl so I can go to court.

Leader: Oh Professor, you're so confused. Kids, some people think that if they just get prayed for at the altar and have a little dab of oil put on their foreheads, they can do anything they want, and God will bless it. They are just as confused as Professor Confuzed. God will give us the strength to do what He wants us to do if we step out on faith and do what we can to obey Him. That is the anointing of God.

Offering: Good Measure Giving

Supplies needed: jar, rocks, sand, water

Read Luke 6:38.

We are talking today about God giving us strength to do what He's called us to do. God also gives us an anointing or the strength to give. When we give in His strength, He blesses us with good measure (show jar and pour in rocks), *pressed down* (pour sand into the jar), *shaken together* (shake jar to settle everything), *and running over* (pour in water).

Bible Story Skit: Bible Time Wrestling – David Verses Goliath (1 Samuel 17)

Supplies needed: Slingshot (optional), five pieces of paper wadded up to be stones, theme music to Rocky (optional)

You will also need two people for this skit. David should be a child or a small teen. Choose a very large or tall man in your church to be Goliath. Have a lot of fun with this skit.

Play theme to Rocky as actors come in. (optional)

Leader: In this corner, standing 10 feet tall and weighing 7 tons, the reigning Philistine champion, who's never been defeated, let's hear it for Goliath.

Goliath enters acting like an arrogant wrestler. Encourage the children to boo.

Leader: And in this corner, standing 4 feet tall and weighing 87 pounds with rocks in his pocket – he's killed a lion and he's killed a bear – let's hear it for the Israelite challenger, David.

David enters acting like a little puny wrestler. Encourage the children to cheer.

Leader: We are proud to present Bible time wrestling. Now David, Goliath, you know the rules. However loses this match, not only does he die, but his entire nation becomes slaves to the champion's nation.

Goliath: Am I a dog that you come to me with sticks. You're toast, David. I'm gonna feed your sorry carcass to the animals when I get done with you.

David: You haven't just come against me, Goliath. You're rumbling with God. I'm gonna cut off your head and feed it to the dogs. You're messin' with the wrong shepherd boy. You want some. Come on.

Goliath laughs uncontrollably and keeps laughing.

Leader: Now the match begins.

As Goliath keeps laughing, David takes a wad of paper (stone) out of his pocket and shoots with his sling shot at Goliath. Optionally, David could throw the papers. Goliath falls down dead.

Leader: The new and reigning champion is David. David could win against the giant because he had the power and anointing of God. He could do all things through Christ who strengthened him.

Praise Break: Tehillah (Use Building a Place for God's Glory lesson 6 praise slide)

This week, during the praise break, children will be learning the next word for praise in the Bible and what it means. Have the children repeat the word Tehillah (pronounced tahela).

Tehillah means to praise God with singing. It's used in Psalm 35:28. "My tongue will speak (or sing) of your righteousness and of your praises all day long."

Have the children give testimonies about things they are thankful for.

Praise and Worship: Choose a couple of fast song and a slow song to lead children into praise and worship. It works well to talk to the children about what worship is and why it's important before you enter into this time. You can have a children's praise team, but until they understand leading praise and worship, have an adult leader or yourself be the worship leader.

Object Lessons:

1. The Candlestick

(Use Building a Place for God's Glory lesson 6, slide B)

Supplies needed: candlestick, candle, lighter

(Show slide B) *In the tabernacle, the golden candlestick represents the Holy Spirit. Last week we talked about the cups on the candlestick and how they represent the fruit of the Spirit. In those days, people didn't have wax candles like this one.* (show candle and light it) *In order to light the candlesticks, each cup had to be filled with oil. Then the candlestick would give light as long as there was oil to burn. In a way, the oil gave the candlestick the power to burn.*

God wants to fill us with the Holy Spirit. As long as we allow the Holy Spirit to fill us, He gives us all the power we need to do what God wants. That's why David had the strength to defeat the giant. He didn't rely on His own strength. He counted on the strength God gave him through the Holy Spirit. It doesn't matter how weak you are. God give you the power you need. Isaiah 41:29-31 says, "He gives power to the weak, and to those who have no might he increases strength. Even the youths shall faint and be weary, and the young men shall utterly fall, but those who wait on the Lord shall renew their strength; they shall mount up with wings like eagles, they shall run and not be weary, they shall walk and not faint."

Not only that, but He will help us through difficult times. Psalm 46:1 says, "God is our refuge and strength, an ever-present help in trouble."

What is really cool is how we get strength from God. When God fills us with the Holy Spirit, He fills us with His joy. Nehemiah 8:10 says, "The joy of the Lord is your strength." That means the more we are filled with God's Spirit, the more He fills us with His joy, and when we are filled with God's joy, we have all the strength we need.

2. Lies that Block God's Anointing

Supplies needed: three poster board with the following written on them or three pieces of flash paper. #1- I'm not old enough to be used of God. #2 - I'm not good enough to be used by God. #3 - I don't have enough faith

If you wish to use flash paper, you can purchase it at magic shops or Google it to make your own.

The anointing of God is the power of God on you to do whatever God wants you to do. He gives you power to live the Christian life, power to minister to people and power to pray for people. But the devil would like children to believe that God won't anoint them or give them power. There are three lies that the devil tells most children when they want to do something for God.

Show first poster or flash paper. *I'm not old enough to be used of God is the first lie the devil will use. He even tries to convince grown-ups that children are too young for the things of God. But that's not what the Bible says. Joel 2:28 says "I will pour out my Spirit on all people. Your sons and daughters will prophesy, your old men dream dreams, your young men will see visions." God didn't say that He would pour out His Spirit on just children. He will pour out His Spirit on all people. Children will prophesy according to this verse. Nobody is too young for God to use.* Light flash paper or tear up poster.

Show second poster or flash paper. *I'm not good enough to be used by God. That is another lie God tells children and adults. God is sad when we sin. But if we ask Him to forgive us, He not only forgives us, but He forgets our sin and removes it from us. God uses people who make mistakes. Peter denied Jesus and God used Him. David stole another man's wife and God used him. Paul killed Christians and God used him. Abraham lied and God used him. The reason God could use these men when they made mistakes is because they asked God to forgive them and they knew that God still loved them and wanted to use them.* Light flash paper or tear up poster.

Show third poster or flash paper. *I don't have enough faith. This is the biggest lie the devil tells children. In Matthew 17:20, Jesus said that God can use even faith that is as small as a mustard seed. A mustard seed is the smallest seed that there is. Most people have at least that much faith, but even if you don't you can ask God to give you faith to believe that He can give you strength to do what He wants you to do. You can also increase your faith by listening to God's Word. Romans 10:17 tells us "Faith comes by hearing, and hearing by the Word of God."* Light flash paper or tear up poster.

The devil never has enough power to defeat the power of God within you.

Message: Smeared with God's Oil

Supplies needed: bottle of oil, plastic sheet or plastic pool

Prepare ahead of time to have a teenager or older child demonstrate having oil poured on him. The student can wear something to keep the oil from getting in his hair. He also should have a change of clothes.

The word anointing comes from a word that means rubbed on or smeared on. When David was anointed to be king, Samuel poured oil on his head and rubbed or smeared it on his head. There is no power in the oil, but it represents the Holy Spirit. The Holy Spirit filled David and gave him the power he needed to defeat Goliath and to be a great king.

Have the student volunteer come forward. Talk about how you are going to demonstrate with your volunteer. Pour about a half bottle of oil over the student's head. Then lay hands on the student and rub in the oil. Pray for the joy of the Lord to be the student's strength. Pray for the protection, strength, and power of the Holy Spirit to overshadow the student. Pray for the student to be filled with the Holy Spirit to overflowing.

Have all of the children come to the altar. Tell them you will anoint them with only a drop of oil, but it doesn't matter how much because it is a symbol of the Holy Spirit.

Tell the students how certain things might happen when they are anointed. They might laugh since the joy of the Lord is their strength. They might be baptized in the Holy Spirit and speak with other languages. They might fall down. Make sure they know there will be catchers if they do. If someone falls out in the Holy Spirit, that person won't get hurt. The catchers are to help the students be more comfortable with what the Holy Spirit wants to do. Let the students know they might not have anything outwardly happen, but they might feel the presence of the Holy Spirit, and they might feel the peace of God come over them. Whatever happens, assure them it's okay.

Anoint each child's forehead with oil and pray for the anointing of God to be on him or her. Don't hurry, and don't try to come up with words for long prayers. Just stand there with your hand on each student's head until God moves. Then when you feel released, go to the next student. If you know the song, end with leading the children to sing *If You Can Use Anything Lord, You Can Use Me*.

Small Group Chat: The Anointing

Talk about what happened during prayer time. Ask the students what they need God's power for. Let them know they have received that power. Have them record their experiences in their journals.

Building a Place for God's Glory Lesson 6

The Oil of Anointing Family Devotions Handout

Memory Verse: Philippians 4:13 NKJV *I can do all things through Christ who strengthens me.*

Summary: We sometimes don't realize how much power we have available to us through the anointing of the Holy Spirit.

This sheet is provided to help families with devotions to go with the lessons your children learned in children's church this week. Included is a daily Bible reading to use for discussions.

Monday: Read 1 Samuel 17:51. Talk about how God gave David the power to defeat a giant.

Tuesday: Read Isaiah 41:10, 29-31. God gives strength to the weak.

Wednesday: Read Nehemiah 8:10. We have strength when God fills us with His joy.

Thursday: Read Joel 2:28. God gives children power and anointing to be used in ministry gifts.

Friday: Read I Chronicles 16:11. We find strength in God when we seek His face.

Saturday: Read 1 Samuel 16:13. David was a great king because the Spirit of the Lord anointed him. The spirit of the Lord anoints all of those who are saved by Him.

Family Activity: Anointing the Sick

Supplies needed: handkerchiefs or small pieces of cloth, olive oil

As a family, anoint the handkerchiefs and pray for the person who receives them to be healed. If you know someone who is sick, give a handkerchief to that person. If not, take the handkerchiefs to a nearby nursing home. Encourage your children to ask the residents if they can pray for them.

Lesson 7: The Gifts of the Holy Spirit

Focus Point: The Holy Spirit operates through the believer with gifts and manifestations.

Goal: Children will know that the Holy Spirit wants to operate in the gifts through them.

Focus Verse: *For this reason, I remind you to fan into flame the gift of God, which is in you through the laying on of my hands.* 2 Timothy 1:6

Supplies needed:

- Building a Place for God Videos (free with registration)
- Building a Place for God Jpeg Slides (free with registration)
- copies of Building a Place for God Family Devotional Sheet
- Professor Confuzed costume: lab coat or a shirt with a pocket protector
- 2 hats
- 2 shirts
- 2 ties
- 2 jackets
- 2 large pairs of pants
- two wrapped gift boxes: one with a rubber snake and one with a rubber or toy scorpion
- special snacks like cupcakes, cookies, candy bars, or donuts

Opening: *Building a Place for God's Glory Countdown* or *Building a Place for God's Glory* Intro Slide (Available free with registration of this curriculum.)

Welcome: *God does great and mighty miracles every day.* Talk about a miracle God has done in your life. Ask the children to tell you miracles that they know about.

Prayer: Ask a child to pray over the service.

Rules: (use rules slide)

Go over the *5 Ups Rules*: 1. Sit up straight. 2. Listen up. 3. Hush up. 4. Don't get up and run around or go to the bathroom. 5. Worship Up! (stand and participate during praise and worship)

Theme or Activity Songs: Choose one or two fast moving activity songs that goes with the curriculum.

Game Time: Clothing Relay (use game time slide)

Supplies needed: 2 hats, 2 shirts, 2 ties, 2 jackets, 2 large pairs of pants

How many of you put on clothes in the morning? Everybody does unless they sleep in their clothes. Nobody likes to see people out at Walmart in the pajamas they've slept in the night before. It is not only

important to put clothes on in the morning. It's also important to be clothed with the power of the Holy Spirit. Today, we are going to see how good you are at putting on clothes.

You will want two teams, one on each side of the room. Choose one person from each team to dress. Each article of clothing will be passed from one member of the team to another. When it gets to the last person, that person runs the article of clothing to his teammate in the front who then puts on the clothing. The first person to put on all the clothing wins.

Memory Verse: *For this reason, I remind you to fan into flame the gift of God, which is in you through the laying on of my hands.* 2 Timothy 1:6

Memory Verse Talk: (use Building a Place for God's Glory lesson 7, slide A)

How many of you have ever seen someone start a campfire? Allow the children to answer. *Sometimes when you start a campfire, you need to blow on it or fan it. That's because a fire needs oxygen. Even if you have a flame, heat, and fuel, if a fire doesn't have oxygen, it will go out. That's why second Timothy 1:6 tells us to fan the flame of the gift of God. God wants to work through us through the Holy Spirit, but if we don't yield to Him and allow Him to work through us, that flame inside us will eventually go out.*

Memory Verse Activity: Memory Verse Tap

Have the students form a circle. They can sit on the floor, stand, or sit in chairs. The leader will walk around the circle. The leader sets his hand on a random student, and that student has to say the next word in the verse. Keep playing until every has a chance and the verse has been completed.

Offering: Gifts to God

Supplies needed: money, calendar

God loves to lavish His love on us through His gifts. He gives us the free gift of salvation, the free gift of the Holy Spirit, and spiritual gifts, and He blesses us with much more. There are also gifts we can give to Him. Here are a few of them.

Show money. *We can give in the offering. God doesn't need our money, but when we give, we show that all we have belongs to Him.*

Show calendar. *We can give God our time. We do this when we go to church or read our Bible, or when we minister to other people. When we give our time, we show that all of our life belongs to Him.*

Raise hands in the air. *We can give God our worship. When we worship God, we show Him that He is worthy of all of our worship.*

Video: Buying Shoes

(Available free with registration of this curriculum.)

Bible Story: Paul and John's Disciples (Acts 19)

Tell this story in your own way.

There are a lot of Christians who don't know about the gifts of the Holy Spirit or the baptism of the Holy Spirit.

Paul ran across Christians like that too. In Ephesus, Paul met some believers who had been baptized by John the Baptist but hadn't ever been taught more. Paul lay hands on these believers, and they were baptized in the Holy Spirit and began to prophesy. That isn't all. Paul preached in that town for months and amazing things happened. God did miracles through Paul. Even handkerchiefs and aprons that Paul had worn were taken to the sick, and the sick were healed. Paul even cast out evil spirits in some of the people there.

You can be a Christian without ever experiencing the baptism of the Holy Spirit or the gifts of the Holy Spirit. The Christians in Ephesus were like that before Paul came, but they also never experienced the miracles and amazing wonders of God. I'd rather experience it all. I want to fan the flames of the gifts of the Holy Spirit in my life.

Praise Break: Shabach (Use Building a Place for God lesson 7 praise slide)

This week, during the praise break, children will be learning the next word for praise in the Bible and what it means. Have the children repeat the word shabach (pronounced shabak).

Shabach means to shout praises to God. It's used in Psalm 47:1. "Shout to God with cries of joy." Have the children shout, "Praise the Lord" together.

Have the children give testimonies about things they are thankful for.

Praise and Worship: Choose a couple of fast song and a slow song to lead children into praise and worship. It works well to talk to the children about what worship is and why it's important before you enter into this time. You can have a children's praise team, but until they understand leading praise and worship, have an adult leader or yourself be the worship leader.

Object Lessons:

1. **The Gift**

Supplies needed: two wrapped gift boxes: one with a rubber snake in it, the other with a rubber or toy scorpion

Jesus once told His disciples about a son who asked his father for a loaf of bread. The father decided to give a gift to his son. What do you suppose he gave him? Do you think the father gave his son bread? Allow the children to answer. Have two children open the gifts. Ask all the children if they think the father would give his son a snake or a scorpion.

Jesus went on to tell the people that if an earthly father wouldn't give his son a scorpion or a snake when he asked for bread, then God will not give us anything bad when we ask for the gift of the baptism of the Holy Spirit. He wants to baptize us with His Spirit so that we can have power to minister in the gifts of the Spirit.

2. Holy Spirit Fire

(Use Building a Place for God's Glory lesson 7, slide B)

For the last two weeks, we have been talking about the golden candlestick that represents the Holy Spirit. We talked about how the cups show us the fruit of the Holy Spirit and last week we learned that the oil shows us that the anointing of the Holy Spirit is there to strengthen us to do God's will.

Today we are going to talk about the flames on each candleholder. They represent the gifts of the Holy Spirit that work through Christians. These gifts are Word of Wisdom, Word of Knowledge, Discernment of Spirit, Miracles, Faith, Healing, Speaking in Tongues, Interpretation of Tongues and Prophecy.

God uses us to work show these gifts in people's lives. The most important gift of the Spirit He will give us is the baptism of the Holy Spirit. When we are baptized in the Holy Spirit, the first thing that will happen is that we will begin to speak in other tongues or in languages we don't know.

Message: The Gifts

(Use Building a Place for God's Glory lesson 7, slides C, D, E, and F)

God uses the gifts of the Holy Spirit in believers so that He can use Christians to minister to others. He never gives the gifts of the Holy Spirit so that the Christian can brag and say, "Look at how special I am." He wants us to glorify Him by helping others with the gifts He gives.

(Show slide C) The most important gift of the Holy Spirit is the baptism of the Holy Spirit. Every Christian who wants to be baptized in the Holy Spirit can be. Just like salvation, the baptism of the Holy Spirit is a free gift that we must accept by faith. If you want to receive the baptism of the Holy Spirit then you can.

(Show slide D) First you must make sure that you are right with God. If you have never received salvation, you must be saved before you can go any further. If you have sin in your life, ask God to forgive you and cleanse you.

(Show slide E) Next ask for the gift. Remember God loves you and wants to give you the Baptism of the Holy Spirit.

(Show slide F) Start worshiping God using your voice. God will never force you to speak, but as you yield your words to Him, He will speak using your voice.

(Show slide G) Have faith. Know that God will baptize you in the Holy Spirit whether he does today, next week or next year. Keep seeking Him.

After you have done all that, praise Him out loud for answering your prayers and if your words start to stammer, then let God's words come out of your mouth.

Give an altar call for those children who would like to receive the baptism of the Holy Spirit. Anoint each child with oil and lay hands on him or her. Speak over each of them something like, "Receive the Holy Spirit." Have children who have received the baptism come up and pray for them.

Small Group Chat: Gift Snacks

Supplies needed: special snacks like cupcakes, cookies, candy bars, or donuts

Today, have a special snack like cupcakes, cookies, candy bars, or donuts. Tell the students you wanted to buy them a gift. While they are eating their snacks, review all the gifts of the Spirit and tell what the gift means. After reviewing each gift, ask them if they have any questions or if God has ever used them in that gift.

Word of Wisdom – God gives us wisdom for a certain situation.

Word of Knowledge – God gives us knowledge we couldn't possibly know on our own.

Discernment of Spirits – God shows us if something is of God, of the devil, or the person faking it.

Miracles – God uses someone to do a supernatural miracle.

Faith – God gives someone faith for something he normally didn't have.

Healing – God uses someone to pray for someone else's healing.

Speaking in Tongues – This is different than praying in tongues. This is giving a group of people a message from God in a language they don't understand.

Interpretation of Tongues – This is the interpretation of the message in tongues.

Prophecy – When God gives you a word or message for someone else.

Building a Place for God's Glory Lesson 7

The Gifts of the Holy Spirit Family Devotions Handout

Memory Verse: 2 Timothy 1:6 *For this reason I remind you to fan into flame the gift of God, which is in you through the laying on of my hands.*

Summary: God uses His gifts through us to minister to others.

This sheet is provided to help families with devotions to go with the lessons your children learned in children's church this week. Included is a daily Bible reading to use for discussions.

Monday: Read 1 Corinthians 12:4-11. Each spiritual gift is important to the body of Christ.

Tuesday: Read Acts 19:1-7. Paul thought it was important for these believers to be baptized in the Holy Spirit.

Wednesday: Read Acts 19:11-12. What gifts of the Spirit were used by Paul in these verses?

Thursday: Read Luke 11:11-13. God will give his children the baptism of the Holy Spirit.

Friday: Read 1 Corinthians 14:39-40. What gift does Paul tells us not to forbid?

Saturday: Read Acts 11:15-18. Talk about the importance of being baptized in the Holy Spirit.

Family Activity: Gifts

Supplies needed: one gift bag for each child with nine small gifts inside

God talked about nine gifts of the Holy Spirit. Give each child one gift bag. Have them talk about each gift they received. Ask them what they had to do to receive these gifts. Remind them that in the same way God wants to give us His gifts including the baptism of the Holy Spirit.

Lesson 8: PUSH - Pray Until Something Happens

Focus Point: The altar of incense teaches us that God hears our prayers and wants us to keep praying.

Goal: Children will learn to keep praying for their needs and for the needs of others until something happens.

Focus Verse: *Continue to ask, and God will give to you. Continue to search, and you will find. Continue to knock, and the door will open for you.* Matthew 7:7 ICB

Supplies Needed:

- Building a Place for God Videos (free with registration)
- Building a Place for God Jpeg Slides (free with registration)
- copies of Building a Place for God Family Devotional Sheet
- Professor Confuzed costume: lab coat or a shirt with a pocket protector
- 1 balloon for each child
- picture of Abraham Lincoln
- camera film
- paper

Opening: *Building a Place for God's Glory Countdown* or *Building a Place for God's Glory* Intro Slide (Available free with registration of this curriculum.)

Welcome: *Today, we are talking about prayer. Many children try praying for something once or twice and if they don't get it, they stop praying. But if they want a certain present for their birthday, they will keep bugging their parents over and over again. Have any of you ever asked your parents for something more than one time. God wants us to do that in prayer. He wants us to not give up. He wants us to push. Push stands for Pray Until Something Happens. God wants us to pray until something happens. When you pray, push.*

Prayer: Ask a child to pray over the service.

Rules: (use rules slide)

Go over the *5 Ups Rules*: 1. Sit up straight. 2. Listen up. 3. Hush up. 4. Don't get up and run around or go to the bathroom. 5. Worship Up! (stand and participate during praise and worship)

Theme or Activity Songs: Choose one or two fast moving activity songs that goes with the curriculum.

Game Time: Push Until Something Breaks (use game time slide)

Supplies needed: One balloon for each child.

When we pray, we must never give up of stop until something happens. We're going to play a game. Each child will receive a balloon. When I say go, blow up the balloon until one child's balloon breaks. That child is the winner.

Give each child a balloon. If a child is afraid of the balloon popping, don't require that child to participate. When a child's balloon pops, that child is the winner. If anyone stops blowing up his balloon, encourage that child to continue until something happens.

Memory Verse: *Continue to ask, and God will give to you. Continue to search, and you will find. Continue to knock, and the door will open for you.* Matthew 7:7 ICB

Memory Verse Talk: (Use Building a Place for God lesson 8, slide A)

Supplies needed: a picture of Abraham Lincoln

When I was in school, I learn about a great president, Abraham Lincoln. Have any of you learned about him? Let the students tell you what they know about Abraham Lincoln.

Abraham Lincoln was president over one hundred years ago. God used him in a great way at a time when the United States was in a war called the Civil War. Because of President Lincoln, the country survived, and slavery ended, but I think the thing that I liked the best about him was that he never gave up.

When Abraham Lincoln was young, his mother died, his sister died, and he had to work to support his family after they lost their home. He failed at business. He lost his job and couldn't get into law school. Then his fiancée died, and he had a nervous breakdown. He spent six months in bed, but he didn't give up. He ran for the state legislator and lost twice. He ran for Congress and lost three times. He ran for senator and lost twice. When he ran for vice-president, he got less than 100 votes.

President Lincoln never gave up. He believed he was supposed to be the president of the United States, and he kept praying and running for office no matter how bad things got. Then in 1860, Abraham Lincoln was elected as the 16th president of the United States.

When we pray, we should act like President Lincoln. Continue to ask, seek and knock in prayer until something happens. When we don't give up, God answers our prayers.

Memory Verse Activity: Ask, Seek, Knock

Divide the students into two teams. The first team says the first part of each section of the verse, and the second team answers.

First Team: *Continue to ask,*

Second Team: *and God will give to you.*

First Team: *Continue to search,*

Second Team: *and you will find.*

First Team: *Continue to knock,*

Second Team: *and the door will open for you.*

After this, switch teams and have the second team go first.

Offering: Testing God

Read Malachi 3:10.

Did you know God wants us to test Him with our tithes? That's right. If we keep on giving our tithe regularly, He promises to provide all our needs and to bless us. That's a test I want to pass.

Puppets or Skit: Professor Confuzed Doesn't Give Up

Professor Confuzed: Hello everyone.

Leader: Hi, Professor Confuzed. I'm glad you made it to church this week.

Professor: I make it to church every week.

Leader: Yes, I noticed that, but I am especially glad that you made it this week because we are talking about something you know a lot about.

Professor: Really, are you talking about electron particles?

Leader: No, Professor, we're not.

Professor: Then maybe you are talking about the mating habits of the mosquito.

Leader: No, we are definitely not talking about the mating habits of the mosquito.

Professor: Then it must be about the effects of cows' burps on the ozone layer.

Leader: Cows' burps? I didn't even know cows burp.

Professor: Then you are confused. You called me just in time. I know all about cows' burps.

Leader: Professor, you're the one who's confused. That's not what we are talking about.

Professor: Then what are you talking about?

Leader: We are talking about prayer and how you should never give up praying until something happens.

Professor: That is true. That is something I know a lot about.

Leader: Tell us about it, Professor.

Professor: Well, I was saved in children's church when I was eight years old. A friend brought me to church because my mom and dad weren't saved. When I got saved, I told my mom and dad how they needed to be saved too, but they were angry with me and told me that I couldn't go back to that church. I prayed every day for my mom and dad to be saved. I also prayed for God to change their minds about me going back to church. Three months went by and nothing happened.

Leader: Did you give up praying?

Professor: Nope, I prayed even harder. Finally, after four months, they started letting me go back to church.

Leader: That's awesome.

Professor: That's not all. Two months later, they started going to church with me, and they became Christians.

Leader: Because you kept praying.

Professor: And praying, and praying, and praying, and praying –

Leader: Until something happened.

Professor: Until the best thing of all finally happened.

Leader: Thanks for telling us your story, Professor.

Professor: Anytime. Would you like to hear more about burping cows?

Leader: Maybe some other time. I'm sure you have somewhere you have to be.

Professor: (looks at watch) Oh, my. I'm late. I have a lab with my students every day at this time. Gotta run.

Leader: Do you think I should let him know he doesn't have lab classes on Sunday?

Bible Story: Daniel's Prayers (Daniel 6, 9, and 10)

Have children volunteer for the following parts: Daniel, 2 royal administrators, 2 guards, King Darius, Angel Gabriel. If you have enough students, also have a couple of them play the part of lions. Instruct the other children to say, "Daniel prayed" every time you have Daniel pray. As you tell the story, have the actors act it out.

In the Old Testament, Daniel was a man of prayer. Every day, he would open his windows and pray. He didn't only pray once. He prayed this way three times a day. (Have Daniel kneel, and the children say, "Daniel prayed." Then have Daniel get back up.)

The royal administrators hated Daniel because they were jealous. They decided to try to get Daniel in trouble. They went to King Darius. They told the king how great he was and asked him to write a royal law that nobody could pray or ask anyone anything but the king for 30 days. King Darius was flattered. He made a decree. Anyone who prays or asks anyone anything for the next thirty days will be thrown in the lion's den to be eaten up.

Daniel found out about the law and about the lions. The royal administrators waited outside his window to see what he would do. Daniel opened the window and prayed three times a day as usual. (Have Daniel kneel, and the children say, "Daniel prayed." Then have Daniel get back up.)

The royal administrators ran to the king and told him what Daniel had done. The king sent the guards to arrest Daniel. When Daniel was brought before the king, the king asked him if he knew about the law. When Daniel said he did, King Darius knew he had no choice but to throw Daniel into the lion's den. King Darius was very sad about this.

Daniel was alone in the lion's den, but he knew God would rescue him. He prayed. (Have Daniel kneel, and the children say, "Daniel prayed." Then have Daniel get back up.) *An angel appeared and shut the lion's mouths.*

The next morning, King Darius call out to Daniel, "Did your God save you?" Daniel came out of the den and told the king how God had saved him. The king was so happy, but he was angry at the royal administrators. He had the guards throw them to the lions. The lions attacked them and ate them up.

Daniel kept praying even when it was dangerous. (Have Daniel kneel, and the children say, "Daniel prayed." Then have Daniel get back up.) *Daniel also prayed when it didn't seem like God was answering.* (Have Daniel kneel, and the children say, "Daniel prayed." Then have Daniel get back up.)

A few years later, Daniel asked God to show him what was going to happen to his nation, Israel. (Have Daniel kneel, and the children say, "Daniel prayed." Then have Daniel get back up.) *The answer didn't come, so the next day, he prayed again.* (Have Daniel kneel, and the children say, "Daniel prayed." Then have Daniel get back up.)

He prayed every day until the answer came. (Have Daniel kneel, and the children say, "Daniel prayed." Then have Daniel get back up.) *He kept pressing through. On the twenty-fourth day, the angel Gabriel appeared to Daniel. He told Daniel God heard him the first day, but there was a war in the Heavens to keep the answer from getting to Daniel. Imagine what would have happened if Daniel had given up after the first day.*

Praise Break: Zamar (Use Building a Place for God's Glory lesson 8 praise slide)

This week, during the praise break, children will be learning the next word for praise in the Bible and what it means. Have the children repeat the word Zamar (pronounced za mar).

Zamar means to praise God with musical instruments. It's used in Psalm 57:7. "I will sing and make music (praise)."

Have the children give testimonies about things they are thankful for.

Praise and Worship: Choose a couple of fast song and a slow song to lead children into praise and worship. It works well to talk to the children about what worship is and why it's important before you enter into this time. You can have a children's praise team, but until they understand leading praise and worship, have an adult leader or yourself be the worship leader.

Object Lessons:

1. **The Altar of Incense**

(Use Building a Place for God's Glory lesson 8, slide B)

Supplies needed: camera film (If you don't have film, you can get some at a photo shop or drug store.)

Can any of you can tell me what this is?

Show roll of camera film. *This is a roll of film for a camera. Until the early 2000s, if you wanted to take a picture, you would have to load this film in your camera. The process of taking photographs was invented and in the 1800s. Once you took all of the pictures on the film, you would have to take it to a photo developer. The photo developer processed the film in a darkroom and turned it into a negative. This was a very delicate procedure because if the undeveloped film was exposed to light, you would lose all your photos! Once developed, the negative would then be used to make the prints that people put in picture frames and photo albums.*

For more than 100 years, people had to buy film, send that film off for processing, and make prints, twenty-four pictures at a time, but since digital photography came about. Things got so much easier than. We don't have to take only 24 pictures at a time, and we don't have to wait to have them developed. We can even store them on the computer or on our phone.

The Bible tells us that praying to God used to be a difficult process. People could pray directly, but if they wanted to make sure their prayers were heard, they had to go to a temple and make sacrifices.

Show Slide B. *Then, a priest would take the prayer request of the people into the Holy Place and light incense at the table of incense.*

Now, we can pray directly to God. In Revelation 8:4, the Bible says that our prayers still rise to God like sweet smelling incense.

2. **Hide and Seek**

Supplies needed: None

How many of you like to play hide and seek? Me too. In fact, I'd like to play hide and seek now. I need two volunteers. Set ground rules if there are places children can't hide.

Have the children hide while you count to ten. After you turn around, tell the children to come on out. This is too hard to search for them.

Do you think that game of hide and seek was fun? Have the children answer. *Me either. In order for it to be fun, I needed to keep searching until I found someone. If I had kept searching, I would have eventually found someone.*

God must be frustrated with us sometimes. If we kept on searching through praying to God for what we need, God would answer, and we would find what we are praying for, but many times, we give us too easily.

Message: Keep On Keeping On (Luke 11:5-10)

Christians, years ago, had a saying. They would tell each other, "Keep on keeping on." That meant keep praying and holding on to God. Pray until something happens.

There was once a man named Fred. Fred had some relatives come to visit him in the middle of the night. Fred lived in Bible days. So, he couldn't go to the all-night grocery store of the convenience store to buy some food for them to eat. His wife hadn't gone to the market for a few days, so they didn't have any bread. Fred had an idea. He would go to his friend, Barney's house and ask him for bread.

When Fred got to Barney's house, it was one o'clock in the morning. Barney was already asleep. So, Fred yelled and pounded on the door. "Barney! Barney!"

Finally, Barney came to the window. "Fred is that you? What in the world do you want at one o'clock in the morning?"

Fred yelled up to Barney, "My wife's relatives are in town, and they're hungry. We need some bread to make sandwiches."

Barney yelled down, "Fred, are you crazy? It's one o'clock in the morning. I am not getting dressed and coming downstairs just to get you some bread. I'm going back to bed." Barney closed the window and went back to bed.

Fred kept yelling. "Barney, Barney, I need some bread." Then he would yell some more. This kept up for fifteen minutes. Finally, Fred saw a light come on downstairs. Barney opened the door a crack and threw some bread out to Fred. Then he slammed the door and went back to bed.

If Barney would get up in the middle of the night just to shut Fred up because he wanted to get some sleep, won't God listen to us pray over and over again and answer our prayers because He loves us? Pray until something happens.

Ask children to come to the altar and pray for what they need. Have them also pray for people who are not saved. Instruct them to keep praying until they get an answer. Lay hands on each of them and agree with their prayer.

Small Group Chat:

Supplies needed: Student's journals (paper for those who don't have journals with them)

A great way to pray faithfully is to write in a prayer journal. Have the children write down what they are praying for. Tell them to circle prayer requests as they are answered.

Building a Place for God's Glory Lesson 8

PUSH – Pray Until Something Happens Family Devotions Handout

Memory Verse: Matthew 7:7 ICB *Continue to ask, and God will give to you. Continue to search, and you will find. Continue to knock, and the door will open for you.*

Summary: Most people say a prayer once then give up. The Bible teaches persistence in prayer.

This sheet is provided to help families with devotions to go with the lessons your children learned in children's church this week. Included is a daily Bible reading to use for discussions.

Monday: Read Daniel 6. Daniel didn't even stop praying when the law threatened to throw him to the lions. Then God rescued him.

Tuesday: Read Daniel 9:20-23. Daniel prayed for twenty-four days, and God heard him the first day he started praying.

Wednesday: Read Revelation 8:1-5. Our prayers are placed on the altar of Heaven as incense.

Thursday: Read Luke 11:1-4. Jesus teaches us how to prayer

Friday: Read Luke 11:5-10 God wants us to keep praying until we have the answer.

Saturday: Read Luke 11:11-13. God gives us good things when we pray. He will baptize us in the Holy Spirit.

Family Activity: Family Prayer Walk

Supplies needed: None

Decide as a family where you should pray. Decide what you should agree to pray about. Take a prayer walk together and pray as you walk.

Lesson 9: Worship That Smells Good

Focus Point: God wants children to enter into the Holy of Holies through praise and worship of Him.

Goal: Children will know that God wants children, not just adults to praise and worship Him.

Focus Verse: *God is Spirit, and those who worship Him must worship in spirit and truth.* John 4:24

Supplies Needed:

- Building a Place for God Videos (free with registration)
- Building a Place for God Jpeg Slides (free with registration)
- copies of Building a Place for God Family Devotional Sheet
- Professor Confuzed costume: lab coat or a shirt with a pocket protector
- dry erase board and markers, or sidewalk chalk, or giant post-it notes and markers
- bottle of perfume
- incense
- incense burner

Opening: *Building a Place for God's Glory Countdown or Building a Place for God's Glory Intro Slide* (Available free with registration of this curriculum.)

Welcome: *Today, we are going to talk about worship that smell good to God. That's right. When you worship God, He says that it's a sweet-smelling incense to Him. So, that means that our worship is expensive perfume to God.*

Prayer: Ask a child to pray over the service.

Rules: (use rules slide)

Go over the *5 Ups Rules*: 1. Sit up straight. 2. Listen up. 3. Hush up. 4. Don't get up and run around or go to the bathroom. 5. Worship Up! (stand and participate during praise and worship)

Theme or Activity Songs: Choose one or two fast moving activity songs that goes with the curriculum.

Game Time: We Know Them by the Sound (use game time slide)

Supplies needed: None

If you have a large group, choose five to seven children to come up front. If you have a smaller group of children, give each child a turn. Each child makes an animal sound. The other child gets to guess what kind of animal it is. Encourage the children to make sounds that are easy to recognize.

When all the children have participated, have one child who you have prepared ahead of time, to come forward and yell, "Praise the Lord," and throw his hands in the air. Then declare that you know what sound that is. That's the sound of a child praising God.

Memory Verse: *God is Spirit, and those who worship Him must worship in spirit and truth.* John 4:24

Memory Verse Talk: (Use Building a Place for God's Glory lesson 9, slide A)

Ask the children to explain what this verse means. If they don't understand all of it, explain it to them.

When I was young, Children's Church played a lot of songs from Psalty the Songbook. Psalty had a saying, "You can sing Christian songs 'til you're blue in the face, but if it's not from your heart it's not praise!" That's true about worship too. It's more than singing. Worship has to come from your heart.

Memory Verse Activity: A Picture is Worth a Thousand Words.

Supplies needed: Dry erase board and markers, or sidewalk chalk, or giant post-it notes and markers

Choose students to play. Have some students draw a picture to represent the first part of the verse – "God is Spirit." Have the second group of children draw, "and those who worship Him must worship." The third group will draw, "in Spirit and in truth." Praise all of the drawings.

Offering: Giving is a Way to Worship

Psalm 54: 6 says, "I will sacrifice a freewill offering to you; I will praise your name, Lord, for it is good." When you give an offering to God, you are showing that He is worthy of that offering. It is one way to worship God in Spirit and in Truth.

God wants us to worship when we give an offering to God.

Skit: Bad Smelling Perfume

Professor Confuzed: Hello everyone.

Leader: Hello, Professor Confuzed. I smell something. Do you smell that, Professor?

Professor: What does it smell like?

Leader: It smells kind of sickening sweet. It's really strong. I'm surprised you don't smell it. Wait, I think that smell is coming from you.

Professor: Oh, you smelled my new perfume?

Leader: Professor, you're a man. Why are you wearing perfume? In fact, why are you wearing such strong perfume?

Professor: I want to smell good to God.

Leader: But worship is what smells good to God, not perfume.

Professor: That's why I got strong perfume. I wanted to make sure God smells it. I'm saving time this way. I don't have to spend time worshipping God. I'll just wear this perfume all of the time.

Leader: Professor, you're confused. God doesn't care whether or not we smell good or in your case bad. He cares whether or not we worship. He wants us to spend time worshipping Him. That's what smells good to Him.

Professor: You mean I wasted $2.00 on a gallon of perfume for nothing. God still wants me to spend time worshipping Him.

Leader: I'm afraid so, Professor.

Professor: Well I have to go now. This female skunk keeps following me and I have to figure out how to get rid of her. I think she thinks I'm a skunk.

Leader: Oh, Professor, you're so confused. Many times, people try to take shortcuts instead of spending time with God, but there are no shortcuts to worship.

Bible Story: Expensive Worship (John 12:1-3)

Supplies needed: bottle of perfume

Ask two students to volunteer. Make sure they know they may smell like perfume afterwards. Have one child take off his socks and shoes. Also ask if any students are allergic to perfume. If they are, you may have to forego using perfume. You could use water instead.

A week before Jesus died on the cross, some men threw a party in His honor. All of His disciples and friends were there including Lazarus and his sisters, Mary and Martha. Mary had saved a lot of money and bought a bottle of very expensive perfume.

Hold up the perfume. *In those days, perfume came in bottle that couldn't be opened easily. When you wanted to use the perfume, you had to break the bottle and let the perfume pour out. Most women saved the perfume they bought for their wedding day. I'm sure that's what Mary planned to do.*

Mary was so excited about Jesus being there, she wanted to find an extravagant way to worship Him. Even though the perfume was very expensive, she broke open the bottle of perfume and washed Jesus' feet with it.

Have one student spray some perfume on the other student's feet and rub it in with her hands.

Mary didn't just rub Jesus' feet. After she poured on the perfume, she wiped His feet with her hair. Do you smell the perfume in the air? Mary poured a lot more perfume out. Everyone at the party could smell it.

Dismiss the children. Spray more perfume in the air.

Smell that perfume. Doesn't it smell good. That's the way in smells to Jesus when we worship Him. It smells like the most expensive perfume you could ever buy. This perfume smells good, but our worship smells even better to God.

Praise Break: Yadah (Use Building a Place for God's Glory lesson 9 praise slide)

This week, during the praise break, children will be learning the next word for praise in the Bible and what it means. Have the children repeat the word Yadah (pronounced ya da).

Yadah means to lift your hands in praise to God. It's used in Psalm 28:7. "…With my song will I praise him."

Praise and Worship: Choose a couple of fast song and a slow song to lead children into praise and worship. It works well to talk to the children about what worship is and why it's important before you enter into this time. You can have a children's praise team, but until they understand leading praise and worship, have an adult leader or yourself be the worship leader.

Object Lessons:

1. **Perfume That Smells Good**

Supplies needed: a bottle of perfume.

A woman should give this object lesson.

Today I have a bottle of my best smelling perfume. I wear this perfume on special occasions like when I'm going to a nice restaurant with my husband or when I come to church. I love the way this perfume smells on me.

Through the years, I have received other kinds of perfume from people as gifts. These were people who didn't know what kind of perfume I like. Occasionally, I would wear the perfume I was given as a gift, but I never liked the smell as much. I would always go back to the perfume that I like the most.

Did you know God has a favorite kind of perfume? His favorite smelling perfume is worship. That's right. Worship is a perfume to God. When we worship God, we smell good to Him. Let's all give God worship that smells good.

2. **The Cloud of Worship**

(Use Building a Place for God's Glory lesson 9, slide B)

Supplies needed: incense and incense burner

Show slide, incense, and incense burner. Light the incense.

In the Holy place of the tabernacle was a table with an incense burner on it. This incense burner would create a fog or a cloud. As the priest would burn incense, he would worship the Lord. God would then cover him with the cloud of His glory. Many times, throughout the Bible, when men and women worshipped God, the cloud of worship would appear.

In 2 Chronicles 5:1-14 it says, "The trumpeters and musicians joined in unison to give praise and thanks to the Lord. Accompanied by trumpets, cymbals and other instruments, the singers raised their voices in praise to the Lord and sang: 'He is good; his love endures forever.' Then the temple of the Lord was filled with the cloud, and the priests could not perform their service because of the cloud, for the glory of the Lord filled the temple of God."

Imagine that. Our worship being so heavy and sweet smelling that God covers us with the cloud of His glory to the point where we could even stand up.

If you have ever experienced this, tell the children the story.

Many people today, when they are worshipping God say that sometimes they see a mist or a cloud. I, for one, always look forward to seeing the glory cloud when I worship.

Message: Worship

You've heard a lot about how worship smells good to God, but what is worship. Praise is when we sing about how great God is. Worship is when we give God all the worth that only is due Him. God wants children to worship and praise Him

Psalm 148:12-13 "Young men and women, old men and children. Let them worship the name of the Lord, for his name alone is exalted; his splendor is above the earth and the heavens."

When we worship God, we exalt His name and recognize how great He is. So, in a minute, we are going to worship God. You can sing and not worship. You can bow and not worship. You can raise your hands and not worship. Worship comes from the spirit and gives God the glory due Him. If you are not doing that, you are not worshiping, and it doesn't smell like perfume to God.

When we worship, let's worship in spirit and truth. Let's worship with our whole hearts. It doesn't matter if you sing, stand, kneel, shout, raise your hand, lay on the floor, cry, or laugh. All of those things might happen while your worshipping, but the important thing is to worship with your spirits.

Play worship songs and lead children into worship. If a child doesn't want to worship, have that student sit in the back so he won't disturb the others. As the children worship, when you feel led to, lay hands on them.

Small Group Chat:

At the end of worship time, ask the children what happened? How did you worship? How did it feel? Did God tell you anything? Did anything unusual happen? Have them record in their journals.

Building a Place for God's Glory Lesson 9

Worship That Smells Good Family Devotions Handout

Memory Verse: John 4:24 *God is Spirit, and those who worship Him must worship in spirit and truth.*

Summary: Worship isn't just singing a song. Worship comes from our spirits.

This sheet is provided to help families with devotions to go with the lessons your children learned in children's church this week. Included is a daily Bible reading to use for discussions.

Monday: Read John 12:1-3. Talk about Mary's worship. Did it come from her spirit?

Tuesday: Read John 12:4-8. Judas complained about Mary's worship because he wasn't really worshipping Jesus from his spirit.

Wednesday: Read 2 Chronicles 5:1-4. What happened when the people lit incense and worshipped God?

Thursday: Read Psalm 95:1-7. This passage tells why we should praise and worship the Lord.

Friday: Read Psalm 100. Read this verse out loud as your worship the Lord.

Saturday: Read Psalm 150. Read this verse out loud as your worship the Lord.

Family Activity: Worship Time

Supplies needed: worship music

Spend some time as a family worshipping the Lord.

Lesson 10: The Veil That Blocks Worship

Focus Point: Children should not let anything keep them from worshiping God.

Goal: In Bible days, the veil kept people from worshipping in the presence of God. Today there is a spirit of Michael that keeps people from worshipping in the presence of God.

Focus Verse: *Let us go right into the presence of God, with true hearts fully trusting him...* Hebrews 10:22

Supplies Needed:

- Building a Place for God Videos (free with registration)
- Building a Place for God Jpeg Slides (free with registration)
- copies of Building a Place for God Family Devotional Sheet
- Professor Confuzed costume: lab coat or a shirt with a pocket protector
- obstacle course using chairs and other items
- 15 bowls
- marker
- snacks (animal crackers)
- football
- a curtain on a rod or stand that can be ripped in two

Opening: *Building a Place for God's Glory Countdown or Building a Place for God's Glory Intro Slide* (Available free with registration of this curriculum.)

Welcome: *You all look good today. It's good to tell complement other people. I want each one of you to find someone to say something nice to.* Have the children complement each other.

Do you know that God wants us to praise and appreciate Him? Let's not let anything stop us from worshipping God.

Prayer: Ask a child to pray over the service.

Rules: (use rules slide)

Go over the *5 Ups Rules*: 1. Sit up straight. 2. Listen up. 3. Hush up. 4. Don't get up and run around or go to the bathroom. 5. Worship Up! (stand and participate during praise and worship)

Theme or Activity Songs: Choose one or two fast moving activity songs that goes with the curriculum.

Game Time: Obstacle Relay Race (use game time slide)

Supplies needed: obstacle course (you can create your own using chairs and other items)

Spilt the students line up into two teams at the beginning of the course. The first child in each team runs the course, then the second, etc. The first team to run the course wins.

Many times in life, we try to do something or go somewhere, but something stop us, just like obstacles in this race. Although in life or in a game, things or people can stop us, we must never let anything or anyone stop us from entering into the presence of God.

Memory Verse: *Let us go right into the presence of God, with true hearts fully trusting him...* Hebrews 10:22

Memory Verse Talk: (use Building a Place for God's Glory lesson 10, slide A)

Many times, things and people try to stop us from entering the presence of God. Sometimes your friends will make fun of you if you try to get closer to God. Other times, it's hard to focus on God when you have school, homework, friends, sports, TV, music, lessons and other interests distracting your attention. You might even be embarrassed or afraid that you might do or say something foolish. Children, nothing is important enough to keep you from getting closer to God. God wants you to enter His presence. Hebrews 10:22 says, "Let us go right into the presence of God, with true hearts fully trusting him..."

Memory Verse Activity:

Supplies needed: 15 bowls, marker, snacks (animal crackers)

Preparation: Write each word of the memory verse on each of the bowls and the verse address on the last bowl. Then fill the bowls halfway with a snack. Animal crackers work well.

Have 15 students volunteer. If you have more than 30 students, you could double the supplies and have two teams.

Students must eat all of the snack to reveal the word hidden at the bottom then place the bowl in order with the other bowls to form the verse. Students work together to do this.

Offering: Obstacles to Giving (Mark 10:17-31)

When you decide to give an offering, do you ever think of reasons why you shouldn't? Maybe you want to use the money to buy a video game, or maybe you don't think you have enough money. Maybe you just like your money so much you want to keep it.

These are obstacles to overcome if we want to live for God. In Jesus' day, Jesus came across a rich young man. The man wanted to follow Jesus and asked Him what he should do. Jesus knew his heart. He cared about his money too much. It was an obstacle in the young man's life. Jesus told him to sell everything he had. The man's face grew very sad. He didn't want to give his money away. He walked away and didn't follow Jesus. Let's not let any obstacle get in the way of our giving.

Puppets or Skit: Professor Confuzed Runs a Race

Professor Confuzed: Hello everyone.

Leader: Hi, Professor Confuzed. How was your weekend?

Professor: I was in an obstacle race yesterday.

Leader: Professor, you didn't tell me that you run in races. That's wonderful.

Professor: This was my first race, but I have been training for months. I run 2 miles every morning.

Leader: That's great, Professor. Running is good exercise. So how did you do in the race?

Professor: Not very well, I'm afraid. I was dead last.

Leader: Don't be too hard on yourself, Professor. After all this was your first race.

Professor: I would have done a lot better if they hadn't put all these planks in the middle of the running tracks. Every time I saw one, I would have to stop and move it out of the way. That took a lot of time.

Leader: Professor, I think you're confused. Wasn't this an obstacle race?

Professor: That's right. The flier said it was an obstacle course. I figured that a man named Mr. Obstacle probably owns the racetrack.

Leader: Professor, you are confused. An obstacle race means that there are obstacles or hurdles on the racetrack. Those hurdles aren't supposed to stop you. You are supposed to jump over them.

Professor: Oh, no wonder everyone was looking at me so strangely. I don't think I'm going to run any more races. I just started running a few months ago. I don't want to have to learn to jump too.

Leader: You don't have to learn to jump. There are other kind of races you can run that don't have obstacles. You could run a marathon.

Professor: That's wonderful. Next time, I'll do one of those races. I have to go now. I need to polish my running shoes.

Leader: Children, sometimes people let obstacles block their worship just like Professor Confuzed let the hurdles stop him from winning his races. No matter what obstacles try to block us, we cannot let them stop us from worshipping God.

Bible Story: The Spirit of Michael (2 Samuel 6:14-22)

In Bible days, there was a king named David. David loved God with all his heart. Because of that, God called David a man after God's own heart. David loved to worship God. He didn't care what anyone thought about him. He would praise and worship God anyway.

One day, Israel was celebrating because the Ark of the Covenant was coming into Jerusalem. The Ark of the Covenant was a symbol for the Glory of God. David was so excited that he took off his kingly robes and danced all the way into Jerusalem. While he danced, he praised and worshipped God. God was pleased that David loved Him so much.

Not everyone was pleased. Michael, David's wife, was mad. She didn't think that David should be acting so undignified. She told David that he was being foolish and wasn't acting like a king.

Many times, people or things, or sometimes even our own fear of being foolish, will keep us from praising and worshipping God. These are obstacles we need to overcome.

Michael didn't keep David from worshipping. David told Michael that he would even become more foolish and undignified to worship the Lord. Just as David didn't let Michael stop him from worshipping God, we must never let anything block our worship of God.

Praise Break: Machowl

This week, during the praise break, children will be learning the next word for praise in the Bible and what it means. Have the children repeat the word Machowl (pronounced machowil).

Machowl means to move your feet or to dance in praise to God. It's used in Psalm 150:4. "Praise him with the timbral and dance."

Have the children give testimonies about things they are thankful for.

Praise and Worship: Choose a couple of fast song and a slow song to lead children into praise and worship. It works well to talk to the children about what worship is and why it's important before you enter into this time. You can have a children's praise team, but until they understand leading praise and worship, have an adult leader or yourself be the worship leader.

Object Lessons:

1. **The Obstacles**

Supplies needed: football

Do any of you ever play football? Maybe one of you could help me. There's something about football that I don't understand. Why is it so hard to hold this ball and run to the other side of the field to score a touchdown? I'm in good shape. I could probably run that far.

Have the children answer. If they don't mention it, talk about the obstacles of people on the other team trying to stop them from taking the ball over the goal line.

There are obstacles in worship too. Most Christians want to worship God, but when they try to, all kinds of thoughts will come against them and try to block their worship. A good football player will not let the players on the other team stop him from making a touchdown. God wants us to be the kind of worshippers that will not let anything block us from worshipping Him.

2. The Veil

Supplies needed: A curtain on a rod or stand that can be ripped in two (optional – use Building a Place for God's Glory lesson 10, slides B & C)

(Show curtain or slide B) *In the tabernacle of Moses was a big thick curtain called a veil that kept people from entering into the Holy of Holies where the presence of God was. Only the high priest could ever go into the Holy of Holies, and he could only enter once a year. That is because God cannot allow sin in His presence, but when Jesus paid the price for our sin on the cross, the veil ripped in two, allowing everyone to enter God's presence.*

(Rip the curtain in two or show slide C) *Many never enter into God's presence. They act as if the veil is still there. Let's tear down the veil in our lives that keeps us from God.*

Message: Reasons Why Kids Won't Worship

(Use Kid's Entering God's Presence lesson 10, slides D, E, F, & G)

There are many obstacles children face when it comes to worshipping God. Here are a few of them.

They don't know God. (Show slide D) *If a child isn't a Christian, if they've never asked God to come in and take over their lives, it's difficult to worship. They don't know God, so how can they worship Him. Jesus died on the cross to get rid of that obstacle, so give your life to Him know.*

Some children are embarrassed. (Show slide E) *They are afraid what their friends might think if they worship God. Sometimes they'll worship a little by whispering words, but they act like spies who want to keep it secret that they're worshipping. God says in Luke 9:26, "Whoever is ashamed of me and my words, the Son of Man will be ashamed of them." I sure wouldn't want God to be ashamed of me.*

Some children are stubborn. (Show slide F) *This child is as stubborn as a mule. He knows God wants him to worship, but he doesn't feel like it. In Acts 7:51, it says, "You stiff-necked people, uncircumcised in heart and ears, you always resist the Holy Spirit." Wow, I wouldn't want to be that person. There is hope. If you are like that, you can ask God to forgive you and change you.*

There is one other reason. Some children aren't hungry. (Show slide G) *If you aren't hungry, it is hard to eat. If you aren't hungry for God, it's hard to worship. Spend some time asking God to give you a hunger for Him.*

During response time, ask the children to find a place on the floor to talk to God about the obstacles in their lives. When they are done, instruct them to come to the front and worship. As you feel led, lay hands on children and pray for them.

Small Group Chat:

Ask the children what obstacles they have in their lives that keep them from worshipping God. Have them write those in their journal. Ask them how they could overcome these obstacles.

Building a Place for God's Glory Lesson 10

The Veil That Blocks Worship Family Devotions Handout

Memory Verse: Hebrews 10:22 *Let us go right into the presence of God, with true hearts fully trusting him...*

Summary: God wants us to go into His presence, but sometimes we have to overcome obstacles to do that.

This sheet is provided to help families with devotions to go with the lessons your children learned in children's church this week. Included is a daily Bible reading to use for discussions.

Monday: Read Mark 10:17-31. What obstacle kept the rich young man from following God?

Tuesday: Read 2 Samuel 6:14-19. David worship before the Lord.

Wednesday: Read 2 Samuel 6:20-22. David's wife tried to become an obstacle to David's worship. How did David react?

Thursday: Read Matthew 27:50-54. This is what happened when Jesus died on the cross.

Friday: Read Luke 9:26. How can embarrassment become a hinderance to worship?

Saturday: Read Hebrews 4:14-16. Jesus wants us to come into His presence.

Family Activity: Family Fun Day

Time for another family fun day doing an activity you all enjoy. At the end of the day, tell your children how much you enjoy spending time with them. Then tell them God feels the same way.

Lesson 11: The Mercy Seat

Focus Point: The mercy seat shows us that if we love and worship God, He will have mercy on us just as we need to have mercy on others.

Goal: Children will learn to be merciful to others just as God has been merciful to them.

Focus Verse: *The Lord is gracious and full of compassion, Slow to anger and great in mercy.* Psalm 145:8 (NKJV)

Supplies Needed:

- Building a Place for God Videos (free with registration)
- Building a Place for God Jpeg Slides (free with registration)
- copies of Building a Place for God Family Devotional Sheet
- Professor Confuzed costume: lab coat or a shirt with a pocket protector
- masking or duct tape
- backpack
- heavy things like bricks, rocks, or books marker
- jar or pitcher full of water
- glass
- bowl
- Chinese finger trap
- Banana
- box with a hole cut out on one end

Opening: *Building a Place for God's Glory Countdown or Building a Place for God's Glory Intro Slide* (Available free with registration of this curriculum.)

Welcome: *Most people don't really understand what mercy is. Mercy is not the same as grace. Grace is the wonderful things God does for us even though we don't deserve it. Mercy is not getting what we deserve.*

For instance, if your mom was driving down the road in a school zone at 70 miles per hour and the police stopped her, what would happen? Let the students answer. *Your mom would probably get a traffic ticket because that's what she deserved, but if the police officer decided to let her go without the ticket, that would be mercy.*

If you were cheating on a test in school and your teacher caught you, what would happen. Let the students answer. *If the teacher said, "I'll let it go this time," and didn't do anything about it, that would be mercy.*

We all have done things to violate God's law. We've cheated, lied, disobeyed out parents, been mean to others, yet God shows us mercy. Jesus took the punishment for our sins, so God could be merciful to us.

Because He is merciful to us, we should be merciful to others.

Prayer: Ask a child to pray over the service.

Rules: (use rules slide)

Go over the *5 Ups Rules*: 1. Sit up straight. 2. Listen up. 3. Hush up. 4. Don't get up and run around or go to the bathroom. 5. Worship Up! (stand and participate during praise and worship)

Theme or Activity Songs: Choose one or two fast moving activity songs that goes with the curriculum.

Game Time: Mercy/Mean Game (use game time slide)

Supplies needed: masking or duct tape

Play this game as you would play Red Light/Green Light, only use the words Mean/mercy. Use tape to mark starting and finishing lines.

Start with everyone along the starting line. When you say "Mercy", everyone will move towards the finish line. When you say "Mean", everyone must immediately stop. If players are still moving when you call "Mean", they must go back to the starting line.

Start a new round when everyone gets across the finish line or when most players make it across the finish line.

Memory Verse: *The Lord is gracious and full of compassion, Slow to anger and great in mercy.* Psalm 145:8 (NKJV)

Memory Verse Talk: (use Building a Place for God's Glory lesson 11, slide A)

God is a merciful God. He loves you and wants you to be His child. No matter what you do in life God will still love you. That's why He sent Jesus, His Only Begotten Son, to die on the cross for your sins. Because He loves you, He wants you to love Him in return. We can let God know how much we love Him by accepting His mercy and forgiveness and by worshipping Him.

Memory Verse Activity: Stand if...

Have the students stand and say the verse if the statements you say apply to them. You can make it as silly as you want. Here are a few examples:

- Took a bath today
- Brushed your teeth today
- Did homework this week
- Talked to a friend this week
- Have a brother or sister
- Have green eyes

End it by having students who have been shown mercy by God stand and say the verse. All of the students should stand.

Offering: Give Because God Has Given to Us

What have you been given to by God? Allow students to answer. If they have a hard time answering, make suggestion such as family, enough food to eat, a home.

We have been given so much by God that we could never repay Him for His mercy. Let's remember that when we give in the offering. We can't outdo God, but we should be so grateful that we want to give.

Professor Confuzed Skit:

Professor Confuzed: (mutters) I can't believe he did that. I'm so angry.

Leader: Hi, Professor Confuzed. What's wrong?

Professor: I was doing research and found a particle that can stop the tendency for cancer in our DNA. It has to be tested yet, but the ramifications are huge.

Leader: Professor, that's wonderful. Are you telling me you found a cure for cancer?

Professor: Not yet, but it's a big step in that direction. This finding could have led to a cure for cancer.

Leader: I don't understand. You seem upset.

Professor: Not upset. I'm so angry.

Leader: But why? Wait a second. You said could have led. What happened?

Professor: I always keep the lab in pristine condition, and I stored the particle in an airtight container in the freezer.

Leader: Yes, so.

Professor: My lab assistance, Edgar, isn't as neat as I am. He was studying the particle. When he finished, he left it out on the table and went home for the day. The cleaning crew came in, dusted, and threw the particle in the trash. The trash was incinerated this morning. Not that it matters. The particle would have been corrupted anyway. It was so inconceivable that my assistant would do that. All this work, all gone.

Leader: I'm so sorry, Professor. Did he apologize?

Professor: Of course, he apologized, but that's not the point. He ruined the experiment. I thought about firing him, but he deserves worse than that. Maybe I should have him categorize all the specimens of dog dodo. Worse yet, I could make him clean the entire lab with his toothbrush then brush his teeth with it. I haven't decided how to punish him yet, but whatever I come up with, he deserves worse.

Leader: How did Edgar feel about ruining the experiment and losing the particle?

Professor: I don't see why that matters. Of course, Edgar feels bad. He went on blubbering about how he was the reason cancer wouldn't be cured, but he still needs to be punished. What he did is unforgivable.

Leader: Professor, have you ever made a mistake?

Professor: Yes, a few, but I didn't destroy the cure for cancer.

Leader: I remember a year ago you telling me that you couldn't form an antiviral medicine because you accidently put the virus in the microwave instead of the refrigerator.

Professor: Oh, well, that's different. I was confused.

Leader: I remember you telling me that the head of the research department forgave you of your mistake and didn't fire you. In fact, that's why you started keeping such a meticulous lab, so you wouldn't make that mistake again.

Professor: What's your point?

Leader: Professor, you're not that confused. You made a huge mistake, and the head of research gave you mercy. Shouldn't you do the same for Edgar?

Professor: I guess you're right. I'll go tell Edgar he doesn't have to categorize fly dung anymore. That's what I made him do until I came up with something worse, but I'll let it go. I'll forgive him.

Leader: I'm glad to hear that. God gives us abundant mercy and forgives all the wrong we've ever done. We should show that same kind of mercy to others.

Bible Story: The Unforgiving Servant (Matthew 18:21-35)

You can use children to act out the parts of this story. Tell the children to be as creative as they want. The four characters needed: the king, the first servant, the second servant, and the jailer.

Once there was a servant of the king named Jim who owed the king more money than he could ever repay. He owed the king millions of dollars. The king called Jim into the royal chamber and demanded that Jim pay back everything he owed.

Jim fell to his knees and cried "Please forgive me. I can't pay back the money I owe. Please don't throw me into jail."

The king was merciful to Jim and forgave him of his debt. The king told him that he did not need to pay back the debt. Jim was overjoyed.

The next day, Jim saw another servant of the king named Sam. Sam owed Jim twenty dollars. Jim went and demanded that Sam give him his money immediately. Sam told Jim that he couldn't pay him back right away, but if Jim would just be patient, he would pay him back. Jim was furious. He ordered the jailer to put Sam in jail until he paid the entire twenty dollars.

When the king heard that even though he had shown mercy to Jim, Jim had not shown mercy to Sam, he became angry. The king ordered the jailer to throw Jim in jail. He also ordered Sam released.

God is like the king in this story. He has shown us mercy and has forgiven us a debt we can never repay. He expects us to show mercy to those who treat us badly.

Praise Break: Barak (Use Building a Place for God lesson 11 praise slide)

This week, during the praise break, children will be learning the next word for praise in the Bible and what it means. Have the children repeat the word Barak (pronounced baw rak).

Barak means to kneel before God in adoration and praise. It's used in Judges 5:2. "When the princes in Israel take the lead, when the people willingly offer themselves-- praise the LORD!"

Have the children kneel. Lead them in a prayer to surrender to God.

Praise and Worship: Choose a couple of fast song and a slow song to lead children into praise and worship. It works well to talk to the children about what worship is and why it's important before you enter into this time. You can have a children's praise team, but until they understand leading praise and worship, have an adult leader or yourself be the worship leader.

Object Lessons:

1. **The Mercy Seat**

(Use Building a Place for God's Glory lesson 11, slide B)

(Show slide B) *In the Holy of Holies of the Tabernacle is a seat called the mercy seat. This seat has two very large angels made of gold that hover over it. Before Jesus died on the cross, once a year, the high priest would have to take the blood of animals and put it in a bowl and place the bowl on the mercy seat. This blood was to cover the sins of the people, so that God could have mercy on them and forgive them. When Jesus died on the cross, He took His own blood and placed it on the mercy seat.*

Once we accept Jesus in our hearts, God shows his mercy toward us:

He forgives and covers our sins. (Psalm 32:1)

He removes our sins from the East to the West. (Psalm 103:12)

He forgets our sins. (Isaiah 43:25)

He throws our sins into the depths of the sea. (Micah 7:18-19)

His mercy never stops flowing. Leviticus 3:22-23(ICB) says, "The Lord's love never ends. His mercies never stop. They are new every morning. Lord, your faithfulness is great.

2. Weight of Mercy

Supplies needed: backpack, heavy things like bricks, rocks, or books

Ask for a student volunteer. Have the student carry the backpack with the flap open for easy access.

Peter once asked Jesus how often he should forgive. Jesus told him seventy time seven. That's 490 times. It's impossible for anyone to offend the same person 490 times in one days, so Jesus was telling Peter to keep forgiving no matter how long it takes. I believe one reason Jesus answered that way is He knew that if Peter didn't learn to forgive and show mercy like God had shown him, he would continue to carry a heavy weight around.

When we don't forgive, we do the same thing. We may hurt the person we won't forgive, but we forgive ourselves even more.

Place a brick (heavy object) in the bookbag. *If someone says something mean to us and says their sorry, it's like carrying the weight of that on our backs.*

Talk about different offenses and keep placing bricks into the bookbag until the volunteer is weighted down with bricks.

Explain how if we forgive, it's like taking that weight off of us as well as the person we are showing mercy to. Give examples by removing each brick and talking about forgiving that offense.

When all of the bricks are removed, ask the volunteer if the bookbag feels any lighter. Explain how the weight of God's mercy is so much lighter and easier to carry than the weight of unforgiveness.

Message: Containers of God's Mercy

Supplies needed: Jar or pitcher full of water, glass, bowl

In 2 Corinthians 4:7, Paul says that we are like clay jars that hold the treasures of God. Show jar or pitcher. *One of those treasures is mercy. Mercy is God's love and forgiveness toward us.*

Have any of you ever done anything wrong? Has God forgiven you? Because God has forgiven us, we have His mercy inside of us just as there is water inside this jar.

Have any of you ever had someone do something wrong or mean to you? All of us have been mistreated at one time or another. When that happens, it's really hard to forgive the person who mistreated you, but if you have God's mercy inside of you, God wants you to pour His mercy out on other people and to keep pouring it out. Pour water into the glass and keep pouring until it runs over into the bowl.

Give these examples of showing mercy to others for each of these.

We can give mercy to those who don't deserve it.

We can show mercy to those who are in need.

We can show mercy to others by treating others with love.

The first is the hardest. When someone doesn't deserve mercy, it is hard to forgive others, but a container of Gods mercy, you can ask God to help you. Sometimes that's hard to do. Your emotions might get in the way, but you don't have to feel good about a person to forgive him. First ask God to help you forgive as He has forgiven you. Then pray for God to bless that person and to forgive him for what he has done for you. After that, look for ways to be good to that person. Before you know it, you'll feel love and mercy toward that person.

Ask children to come to the altar if they need forgiveness and mercy from God or if they need to show someone else mercy. Lay hands on the children and pray for them.

Small Group Chat:

Supplies needed: Chinese finger trap, banana, box with a hole cut out on one end

Let each child in your group to try the Chinese finger trap. Ask them if they can get their fingers out when they try to pull them out. That's the way it is with unforgiveness. If we struggle against letting go of the offense, we can't break free from it.

Tell the students the following story about the monkey trap.

Hunters in Africa use a very simple trap to capture monkeys. Show box. They use a box similar to this one with a hole on one end barely large enough for a monkey to get its hand through. Show banana. They place the banana inside the box. Demonstrate. The monkey sees the banana and puts his hand inside to get the banana, but he can't get his hand back out. Demonstrate using your own hand. You would think the money would just let go of the banana, but he won't. He'll stay there holding the banana until a hunter comes to get him or until he starves to death.

When we hold onto unforgiveness instead of showing mercy, we are just like those monkeys. We won't let go of the banana.

Building a Place for God's Glory Lesson 11

The Mercy Seat Family Devotions Handout

Memory Verse: Psalm 145:8 (NKJV) *The Lord is gracious and full of compassion, Slow to anger and great in mercy.*

Summary: God is always showing great mercy toward us. Because we have been shown mercy, we should show mercy toward others. Mercy is not getting what we deserve.

This sheet is provided to help families with devotions to go with the lessons your children learned in children's church this week. Included is a daily Bible reading to use for discussions.

Monday: Read Matthew 18:15-22. God has a method to handle those who offend us. We go to them, and then, we forgive them.

Tuesday: Read Matthew 18:23-35. We should show mercy because we have been shown so much mercy.

Wednesday: Read Leviticus 3:22-23. God shows us more love, mercy, and faithfulness than anyone else ever could.

Thursday: Read 2 Corinthians 4:6-9. When we show mercy, we are containers that show God's glory.

Friday: Read Micah 7:18-19. God shows such mercy to us that He throws our sins into the depths of the sea.

Saturday: Read Psalm 32:1. God's mercy covers and forgives our sins.

Family Activity: Forgiveness Prayer List

Supplies needed: poster, marker

Ask your children if they are having a hard time forgiving someone. Parents, include yourself in this list. Write the names down on the poster board. Lead your children in a prayer for God to bless the people on the list. Hang it in a central location so your children can pray for the people on the list every time they pass by. You do the same.

Lesson 12: The Glory of God

Focus Point: Because Jesus died on the cross, we can see the glory of God.

Goal: Children will learn what the glory of God is and desire to see His glory.

Focus Verse: ...*Now, show me Your Glory.* Exodus 33:18 NIV

Supplies Needed:

- Building a Place for God Videos (free with registration)
- Building a Place for God Jpeg Slides (free with registration)
- copies of Building a Place for God Family Devotional Sheet
- Lucy costume: modest outfit you might wear to the beach, sunglass, beach towel
- feathers (enough for each child to have one)
- beachball or playground ball
- blanket
- different size boxes that fit inside each other
- microscope
- telescope

Opening: *Building a Place for God's Glory Countdown or Building a Place for God's Glory Intro Slide* (Available free with registration of this curriculum.)

Welcome: *Many people talk about the Glory of God. Does anyone here know what the Glory of God is?* Give the children a chance to answer. *The Glory of God comes from the word, Kabod which means heaviness. The Glory of God is the awesome heaviness or weightiness of God. There is another word for Glory, Shekhinah. Shekhinah means to reside in or rest upon. We've been talking about the Tabernacle of Moses through the last few weeks. The Tabernacle was the place God's glory or weightiness rested upon or lived in. Today, we don't have a tabernacle we go to find God. When we become Christians, God's glory or weightiness lives inside of us. All we have to do in yield or surrender to His Glory and let His light shine through us.*

Prayer: Ask a child to pray over the service.

Rules: (use rules slide)

Go over the *5 Ups Rules*: 1. Sit up straight. 2. Listen up. 3. Hush up. 4. Don't get up and run around or go to the bathroom. 5. Worship Up! (stand and participate during praise and worship)

Theme or Activity Songs: Choose one or two fast moving activity songs that goes with the curriculum.

Game Time: Breathing (use game time slide)

Supplies needed: feathers

The Holy Spirit lives in us and breathes the glory of God into us. Sometimes the Holy Spirit is called the breath of God. We're going to use our breath in this game.

Give each child a feather. For this game, instruct them to place their feathers on top of their mouths and tilt their heads back. When they hear the word go, they will try to keep their feathers in the air using only their breaths. The last student who still has his feather in the air wins.

Memory Verse: *...Now, show me Your Glory.* Exodus 33:18 NIV

Memory Verse Talk: (use Building a Place for God's Glory lesson 12, slide A)

God is an awesome God. His Glory is more awesome than anything that can be imagined. There is nothing more wonderful than to be in the presence of God and to let His glory rest upon you like a heavy blanket in the winter. Even though God lives inside every Christian, God will not show His Glory to those who are not interested. He wants us to chase after Him and seek Him with everything within us. He wants us to yield to Him and to seek His Glory. He wants us to all pray today's memory verses, "Now, show me Your Glory." Exodus 33:18.

Memory Verse Activity: Memory Verse Beach Ball

Supplies needed: 1 beach ball or playground ball.

Have two children who can recite the memory verse, come up front. Explain to the children that they are to bounce the ball to each other. As they bounce the ball, they are to say the next word of the memory verse until every word of the verse is said. Repeat with two more children as often as you have time for.

Offering: Giving for God's Glory

I Corinthians 10:31 says, "So whether you eat or drink or whatever you do, do it all for the glory of God." That means even when we give an offering, we should do it for the Glory of God. Giving for the glory of God means we give because we love God so much we want to show His glory to everyone. When we give, some of the money we give goes to share the Gospel with people here and around the world.

If your church has a mission's program, this is a great time to talk about missions. You could also tell the students, next week you will have a mission's offering.

Skit: Let the Son Shine

Supplies needed: beach towel

Have a girl come in with a beach towel and lay the towel on the floor. She should then lay down on the towel and act like she is sunning herself.

Leader: Excuse me, miss. We're in the middle of a church service here. What do you think you're doing?

GIRL: I'm soaking up the Son.

Leader: Shouldn't you be soaking up the sun outside? After all that is where the sun is.

GIRL: You don't understand. I'm soaking up the Son of God. A preacher told me that if I want the glory of God in my life, I need to spend every day soaking up the Son of God.

Leader: Are you related to Professor Confuzed by any chance?

GIRL: How did you guess? I'm his daughter. He won't be here today so I'm taking his place. My name is Lucy Confuzed.

Leader: Well Lucy. You are confused. You don't soak up the Son of God the same way that you soak up the sun in the sky.

GIRL: You don't

Leader: No Lucy. You soak up the Son of God by spending time worshipping Him.

GIRL: I guess I am confused. I need to go tell my father. He's the one who told me how to soak up the Son of God.

Leader: Why am I not surprised? Good-bye, Lucy.

Bible Story: Moses (Exodus 20:18-21)

In Moses' day, Moses and the people of God to Mt. Sinai to hear from God. Moses told the people to prepare themselves because God was going to reveal His Glory to them. As the people stood at the foot of the mountain, the Glory of God surrounded the mountain like a thick cloud. God voice thundered on the mountain as He spoke to Moses.

Instead of getting excited and worshipping God and thanking Him for showing them His Glory, the people ran away and told Moses that they wanted Him to tell them what God said. They did not want to get close enough to God to hear His Voice.

The sad part of the story is that even today, God wants to reveal His Glory to His people, but most people do not want to get close enough to God to see His Glory. They want God to save them, and they want God to help them through their troubles, but they don't want God to change them, and they don't want to give up everything for Him. They're afraid God will make them do something they don't want to do or show His glory in a way that makes them uncomfortable.

I never want to be like that. I want to be like Moses.

Lead the children in saying, "Lord, show me Your Glory."

Praise Break: Sachaq (Use Building a Place for God lesson 12 praise slide)

This week, during the praise break, children will be learning the last of the nine words for praise in the Bible and what it means. Have the children repeat the word Sachaq (pronounced sawqua) Sachaq means to laugh. It's used in Proverbs 8:30. "Then I was constantly at his side. I was filled with delight day after day, *rejoicing* (laughing) always in his presence."

Many times, people think to worship God you always have to be serious, but God wants to show us His Glory. He wants us to rejoice in Him. Sometimes that even means laughing.

Praise and Worship: Choose a couple of fast song and a slow song to lead children into praise and worship. It works well to talk to the children about what worship is and why it's important before you enter into this time. You can have a children's praise team, but until they understand leading praise and worship, have an adult leader or yourself be the worship leader.

Object Lessons:

1. The Blanket

Supplies needed: blanket

I want to show you my very favorite blanket and tell you why I like it so much. When I was littler, before I went to school, my mom would have to leave me at the babysitters while she went to work. She went to work very early, and she didn't want me to have to get up that early. So, she would wrap me in a big heavy blanket and carry me to the car. The blanket was so heavy and warm, and it felt so safe. Sometimes, I would wake up while she was carrying me, but I loved the way I felt in that blanket so much that I never let her know that I was awake.

The word glory means heavy. God's glory is like a big heavy blanket that covers us and makes us feel safe. That's why I brought my favorite blanket to show you. God's glory reminds me of my favorite blanket. I want Him to show me His glory just like I'm showing you this blanket.

The Ark of the Covenant

(Use Kid's Stepping Into God's Presence, lesson 12, slide B)

Supplies needed: a number of boxes different sizes that fit inside each other

Today we are talking about the last piece of furniture in the tabernacle. This is the Ark of the Covenant. God, in the Old Testament times, before Jesus died on the cross, showed His Glory and His Awesomeness in the Ark of the Covenant. Because of that, many times the Ark of the Covenant was called the container of God's Glory. God didn't ever want to contain His Glory in a box. From the beginning of time, it has been His desire for the whole Earth to be filled with His Glory. He has always wanted to reveal His Glory to His people. He couldn't do that until Jesus died on the cross for our sins. That's why in John 12:23, "Jesus replied, "The hour has come for the Son of Man to be glorified."

Because of what Jesus did, God's glory isn't contained in a box. God wants to reveal His Glory to all

who are hungry for Him. Unfortunately, Christians still want to keep God's glory in a box and bring it out whenever they need it.

Show boxes. *Some Christians have small boxes that they can carry around with them, and some have great big boxes. The ones with great big boxes are usually proud that they don't keep God in a tiny little box, but God is greater than any box we could ever put Him in.*

Message: The Glory of God

Supplies: telescope, microscope (You may be able to borrow these from a child or adult who enjoys science. If you can't, use pictures you can find online.)

Show microscope. *A microscope shows how we can show the glory of God in our lives. When you study something under a microscope, it makes things appear larger. The more we glorify God, the larger His Glory become in our lives. What are some of the ways we can glorify God?* Allow students to answer, then give your own answers.

Show telescope. *A telescope makes objects that are far away look larger. The more we satisfy ourselves in God, surrender to Him, and worship Him, the greater He will show Himself to us.*

We are going to spend some time worshipping God now and allowing Him to show us His Glory. Sometimes, He'll do that by giving us a great sense of peace. Sometimes we'll want to lie on our faces before God, or we won't be able to stand up. Sometimes we'll dance. Sometimes we'll shout. Sometimes we'll cry. And sometimes we'll laugh. Let's let God do whatever He wants to do in our lives and not put Him in any boxes.

Ask children to come forward if they want God to show them His Glory and they want to get closer to Him. Don't rush this or try to make something happen. Pray for God to show your students His Glory. Then do whatever God leads you to do.

Small Group Chat:

Supplies needed: microscope

Have slides ready and allow each child to look at the slide. Ask the students how something looks different under a microscope than it does normally.

Building a Place for God's Glory Lesson 12

The Glory of God Family Devotions Handout

Memory Verse: Exodus 33:18 NIV …*Now, show me Your Glory.*

Summary: God's Glory is the weightiness or heaviness of the presence of God.

This sheet is provided to help families with devotions to go with the lessons your children learned in children's church this week. Included is a daily Bible reading to use for discussions.

Monday: Read 1 Corinthians 10:31. What should we do for the Glory of God?

Tuesday: Read Exodus 20:18-21. How did the people react to God's Glory?

Wednesday: Read Exodus 33:12-23. How did Moses react to God's Glory?

Thursday: Read Hebrews 1:1-4. Jesus is God's Glory

Friday: Read Isaiah 40. God, show us Your Glory.

Saturday: Read 1 Chronicles 16:8-12. God wants up to worship Him and seek His Glory.

Family Activity: Star Gazing

Supplies needed: telescope (optional)

According to Psalm 19:1, the stars declare the Glory of God. To demonstrate this, take the family outside one night for some star gazing. If you have a telescope, use it and let each child look through it. If you live in the city, this works better if you drive out to the country where the streetlights won't interfere.

Lesson 13: The Revival Harvest

Focus Point: Jesus wants us to be His witnesses to the world so that a revival harvest of souls will be won to Christ.

Goal: Children will learn how to share the gospel with others using the Holy Spirit to guide them.

Focus Verse: *...Go into all the world and preach the good news to all creation.* Luke 16:15 NIV

Supplies Needed:

- Building a Place for God Videos (free with registration)
- Building a Place for God Jpeg Slides (free with registration)
- copies of Building a Place for God Family Devotional Sheet
- Professor Confuzed costume: lab coat or a shirt with a pocket protector
- Fishing pole or picture of a fisherman
- string or tape
- oil lamp or lantern or flashlight
- basket
- post-it notes
- pens
- jewelry cords or vinyl lacing cords (string will also work)
- beads in the following colors: yellow, black, red, white, green

Opening: *Building a Place for God's Glory Countdown or Building a Place for God's Glory Intro Slide* (Available free with registration of this curriculum.)

Welcome:

Supplies needed: fishing pole (optional)

Today, we are going fishing. What are some things people go fishing for? Let the children name some things.

We aren't going fishing for any of these things. God wants Christians to fish for people. You might be wondering how you can possible go fishing for people. We'll talk about that later in the service.

Prayer: Ask a child to pray over the service.

Rules: (use rules slide)

Go over the *5 Ups Rules*: 1. Sit up straight. 2. Listen up. 3. Hush up. 4. Don't get up and run around or go to the bathroom. 5. Worship Up! (stand and participate during praise and worship)

Theme or Activity Songs: Choose one or two fast moving activity songs that goes with the curriculum.

Game Time: Talking to Strangers (use game time slide)

Supplies needed: None

Sometimes it's hard to tell people about ourselves. It's sometimes even harder to tell people about God. We're going to do an experiment. Each child needs a partner.

Give each child a partner that he or she doesn't normally talk to. If there are an uneven number of children, have a worker team with the child that is left. Have each pair decide who will go first.

When I say go, for two minutes, I want you to talk about yourself to your partner. You cannot stop talking until I say stop.

Reverse roles. Have the child who listened, talk this time.

Now we are going to do the same thing again. Only this time, you are going to talk about God instead of yourselves.

How many had an easier time talking about you than about God? How many of you had an easier time talking about God? Lots of people never share their faith with other because they don't know what to say. Later I'm going to teach you an easy way to remember how to share your faith with others.

Memory Verse: ...*Go into all the world and preach the good news to all creation.* Luke 16:15 NIV

Memory Verse Talk: (use Building a Place for God's Glory lesson 13, slide A)

Many Christians are able to boldly proclaim the gospel in church, but out in the world, they become secret agent Christians. Although they live the Christian life, they never tell their non-Christian friends the good news that Jesus cares for them. This is a shame because the Word of God says that we are all to be witnesses of Christ. Mark 6:15 says, "And he said unto them, go ye into all the world and preach the gospel to every creature." Every creature includes your friends, your family, and even people you don't know.

Memory Verse Activity: Gone Fishing Tag

Supplies needed: string or tape

Use the string or tape to draw a large circle in the middle of the room. This game is played like tag, only when someone is caught, he goes to a circle in the middle of the room. The circle is the fishing net. The person who is it is the fisherman. The other students are the fish.

Offering: Missionary Offering

This is a good time to collect an offering for missionaries who share the Gospel around the world.

Puppets or Skit: Professor Confuzed Becomes a Fisher of Men

Professor Confuzed: Hi everyone. I just wanted to let you know that I'm going away for a few weeks on vacation.

Leader: That's great, Professor Confuzed. Where are you going?

Professor: I've decided to go fishing.

Leader: I hope you have a fishing pole this time, Professor.

Professor: Of course, I have a fishing pole. I also have hooks and huge worms.

Leader: Wow, that's fantastic. You're learning to be prepared, Professor. Where are you going fishing?

Professor: New York City.

Leader: New York City seems like an unusual place to go fishing, but it is on the ocean. What kind of fish are you going to try to catch?

Professor: New York City is perfect for what I'm fishing for. I'm fishing for men. There are a lot of men in New York City.

Leader: Are you telling me that you're going to New York City to catch men with a fishing pole and worms?

Professor: That's right. Jesus told us to be fishers of men. Can you think of a better place to fish for men than New York City?

Leader: Yes, Professor, but you don't catch men with fishing poles. Besides most people don't like to eat worms.

Professor: How else am I going to use to fish for men?

Leader: When Jesus told us to be fishers of men, He didn't mean that we should try to catch men with fishing poles.

Professor: Then what did He mean?

Leader: When Jesus said that we should become fishers of men, He meant that we should tell other people about Jesus so that they can be saved.

Professor: Oh, then I better be going now. I need to try to get my deposit back on the fishing boat I was buying.

Leader: Oh Professor, you're so confused. Have fun on your trip.

Bible Story: Power to Witness (Acts 1:8)

(Use Building a Place for God's Glory lesson 13, slides B, C, D, and E)

Acts 1:8 says, "But you will receive power when the Holy Spirit comes on you; and you will be my witnesses in Jerusalem, and in all Judea and Samaria, and to the ends of the earth."

The power we receive is the power of the Holy Spirit. You receive some Holy Spirit power when the Holy Spirit comes to live inside you or when you become a Christian, but you receive so much more power when you become baptized in the Holy Spirit. The Holy Spirit will give you boldness and wisdom to know how to witness. This verse also tells us who to witness to.

(Show slide B) Jerusalem: This was where the disciples lived. So, you should witness where you live: your home, your neighborhood, your school, your sports, dance, or music lessons, or anywhere else you would normally go. You witness to the people you know.

(Show slide C) If you don't live in the United States, find a picture or map of your nation. Judea: This is the country the disciples lived in. We should also witness to our nation. Many of us can't do that, but we can pray for our nation to experience revival and for people to be saved, and we can give money to our church or other ministries that minister to our nation.

(Show slide D) Samaria: These were the outcasts where the disciples lived. In our day, they would include the poor, the destitute, and the homeless. It is important to share the Gospel to the outcasts. One of the most effective ways to do that is to give them what they need: food, clothing, shelter. Then we can show them God loves them and wants them to be saved. One way we could do this is to donate food and clothing to Christian ministries who minister to these people. Another thing we could do is volunteer at one of these places. We could also visit nursing homes and hospitals and share the love of Jesus.

(Show slide E) The ends of the Earth. When you are older, some of you will be called to go to other nations and preach the Gospel. People who do this are called missionaries. Most of you will never live in another country, but you can help missionaries by support them with offerings and prayer.

Ask God how and where He wants you to witness about Jesus and what He has done in your lives.

Praise Break: Glorifying God (Use lesson 13 praise slide)

Today we're going to talk about how we can cause other to praise and glorify God. Matthew 5:16 says, "Let your light so shine before men, that they may see your good works, and glorify your Father which is in heaven."

If you only praise God in church, then people, who don't go to church, will never know God. But if you praise God, by doing good for others and sharing the Gospel, then they will see God in your lives and want to know more about Him.

Have the children talk about how they could praise God by doing good for others.

Praise and Worship: Choose a couple of fast song and a slow song to lead children into praise and worship. It works well to talk to the children about what worship is and why it's important before you enter into this time. You can have a children's praise team, but until they understand leading praise and worship, have an adult leader or yourself be the worship leader.

Object Lessons:

1. Using the Right Bait

Supplies needed: a fishing pole or a picture of a fisherman

This is a fishing pole. You need a fishing pole when you go fishing. If any of you have ever gone fishing, raise your hands. What else do you need when you go fishing? Have the children answer. If bait is not one of the answers, mention it.

What are some kinds of bait that people use when they are fishing to catch fish? Have the children answer. *We can't use the same bait for catching fish that we use for catching people. Not too many people I know like to eat worms, but there is bait that we can use to become fishers of men. That bait is the way we live our lives.*

Matthew 5:16 says "Let your light so shine before men, that they may see your good works, and glorify your Father which is in heaven." If we live our lives so that people can see the light of God in us because of all the good we do and how we love others, they will want to know more about God. That is how we bait them so that we can share the love of God with them.

2. The Lamp (Luke 11:33-36)

Supplies needed: oil lamp or lantern or flashlight, basket

Jesus say that Christians are the light of the world. If you were in a very dark place and the only light you had was this lantern, would you cover the lantern with a basket so that the light couldn't be seen?

Demonstrate by placing the basket over the lantern. *Of course, you wouldn't. You would want the light to burn brightly so that you and everyone around you could see where you are going.*

When you are with your non-Christian friends and you pretend to go along with them when they are talking about doing a thing you know are wrong, or you won't tell them that you love Jesus, you are doing the same thing.

You are the light in a dark world that doesn't know Jesus. Jesus wants you to show your faith in Him and shine brightly in the darkness. When you don't do that, it's like you're putting a basket or a cover over your light and allowing your friends to remain in darkness.

Message: How to Be a Fisher of Men

Supplies needed: witnessing bracelet (see small group activity for how to make a witnessing bracelet), basket from The Lamp object lesson, post-it notes, pens

Lesson 13: The Revival Harvest

Today we are going to learn how to become fishers of men.

If you want to share the gospel, the first thing you must do is let your light shine by the way you act and treat others. Ask God to help others see His light in you. If you do this, your friends might ask you why you are different.

Next pray for your friends and family that aren't saved. Ask God to give them the desire to want to know more about Jesus. Make a prayer list of friends and family you want God to save. Then you can read the list to God every day. Also pray in the Holy Spirit. Ask God to give you boldness and help you to know what to say.

Once you've done that, wait for God to open up doors for you to talk to your friends.

Show your bracelet. *One way to help you talk to your friends about Jesus and salvation is to wear a witnessing bracelet. Each color in the bracelet means a different thing.*

Yellow: God loves us, and He wants us to go to Heaven to be with Him forever when we die.

Black: Even though God loves us, He cannot allow sin into Heaven. Everyone has sinned or done something wrong and so God cannot allow any of us into Heaven to be with Him.

Red: Because God loves us so much, He sent His Son to die on the cross and take the punishment for our sins. Jesus blood washes away our sins.

White: When we ask Jesus to come into our lives, He washes our sins away and gives us a clean heart so God can accept us, and we can become His children and live with Him in Heaven.

Green: God doesn't just want us to go to Heaven. He wants us to grow closer to Him on Earth. We can grow in the Lord by going to church, learning more about the Bible, praying and obeying God's commands.

Ask each student to write a name on a post-it note that he wants to know Jesus. Have him bring that note to the front and place it in the basket. Then have him find a quiet place in the room to pray for the name on the post-it-note.

Small Group Chat: Witnessing Bracelets

Supplies needed: jewelry cords or vinyl lacing cords (string will also work), beads in the following colors: yellow, black, red, white, green

Cut strings in 15-inch lengths. String each bead on the cord. Then tie a knot before placing the next bead on the cord. When all five beads are on the cord, tie the following knot. (You can also use jewelry clasps on each end.)

Take the first end and knot it around the second end.

Take the second end and knot it around the first end.

Building a Place for God's Glory Lesson 13

The Revival Harvest Family Devotions Handout

Memory Verse: Luke 16:15 NIV *Go into all the world and preach the good news to all creation.*

Summary: True revival always includes soul winning. God wants ever believer to be His witness and to share the Gospel with others.

This sheet is provided to help families with devotions to go with the lessons your children learned in children's church this week. Included is a daily Bible reading to use for discussions.

Monday: Read Matthew 4:18-22. Jesus wants us to be fisher of men.

Tuesday: Read Acts 1:8. God gives us power to witness to the people we know, the outcasts, our nation, and our world.

Wednesday: Read Matthew 5:14-16. One way we witness is to let our lights shine.

Thursday: Read Matthew 16:15-18. God will protect us as we are witnessing to others.

Friday: Read Acts 8:30-35. Here is an example of someone witnessing.

Saturday: Read Ephesians 2:8-9. If you want others to understand how to be saved, this verse says it all.

Family Activity: Helping the Least of These

Find a place you can take the entire family to show the love of Jesus. You could visit a nursing home, help an elderly neighbor with yard work, work at a food pantry handing out food, give bottles of water to the homeless, or be creative and think of another way to minister.